T0072504

# Writing Out Loud

A Collection of Literary Expressions

By

C. Allen Berry

Cover and Interior Photos by: Ms. Darcie Huffman and C. Allen Berry



Balboa Press books may be ordered through booksellers or by contacting:

Balboa Press
A Division of Hay House
1663 Liberty Drive
Bloomington, IN 47403
www.balboapress.com
1 (877) 407-4847



Print information available on the last page.

ISBN: 978-1-5043-8850-4 (sc)
ISBN: 978-1-5043-9000-2 (e)

Balboa Press rev. date: 02/28/2018

For Ms. Cynthia…thanks for believing

# Writing Out Loud

# Table of Contents

# Introduction

I love writing. But it wasn't always that way. I started out wanting to be a comic book artist. When I was in junior high, I would often fake being sick just so I could stay home from school and draw and create stories (I think my mother knew, but still indulged me from time to time). I never realized I was writing back then, as my focus was so much on the art. But all that changed my freshman year in a ninth-grade English class when my teacher, a middle-aged white woman with stylish graying hair and a strange affection for Calypso music, gave us the classroom assignment of writing a brief autobiography. What I turned in started like this:

*"I grew up through a maze of comic books and dreams designed to break down the poverty of a childhood existence. Oh, the sweetness of those days, wrapped in bitter melancholy, still stamped upon the envelope of my mind...."*

The next day she took me aside and said that I had a gift for stringing words together, and that I should consider pursuing the ideal of being a writer. I tell this story because I wasn't a good student; at best I was average and borderline failing. For a young black kid coming of age in 1966 at a very tumultuous time in the history of our country, what that teacher said had a very profound effect on me and who I was to become.

This was reinforced several years later in a creative writing class taught by a young, first-year graduate teacher. Fresh out of college and just barely outside my dating range, she taught me metaphor and similes; put the rhyme in alliteration; and personified the language of description in the corrections she made to each bit of poetry and prose I handed in. She kept me from failing high school and sang my praise in a poem that was later published in a small literary magazine. She believed in me as a writer long before I believed in myself.

I read somewhere once that the word educate, at its root, means "to draw out," that the essence of the intellect is already there waiting to be coaxed into being. As the statue residing at the heart of the stone is dependent on the skill of the sculptor to release the image, so too are the aptitudes of the student dependent on the skill of the teacher "to draw out" the best in him/her.

To this day I am indebted to teachers who look beyond the stereotypes, gruff exterior and surly attitude, to recognize the vast potential that resided within; to see the deeper value of the persons placed in their charge. To this day I feel blessed.

I love writing.

I know I'm just repeating myself, but to watch words magically appear across the blank screen of a white page is a very enjoyable experience. For a while I wasn't really sure if I loved the craft enough. I remember the passion I had for it when I was younger and the seeds were first sown, and the sprouts of imagination unfurled themselves to push their way up through the hard soil of grit and grammar, and between the cracks of writer's block.

In those days I feasted on writing as if it were a final meal or some forbidden fruit I had never tasted before. Locked away in the hot, shadowy comfort of my attic room, I'd sit hunched for hours over the small keyboard of my older brother's portable gray typewriter, plotting and pecking out the drama of make-believe lives.

I think that's what I love most about writing. The fact that I get to fool around with history —that of others as well as my own—and that I get to weave it into a pattern of a whole other reality and come up with a garment of my own design. If I do this skillfully enough, I give answer to the secret musings we've all had at one time or another of asking, "What if?" What if things had been different and I had been born a girl…or a different color…or on a different continent? My God, I can only imagine…but as a writer I get to do more than just imagine. I get to make it so.

I no longer doubt my love for the craft. Though not as all-consuming as it once was—when I was just an ingénue in that shadowy closed-off attic—the passion is still there; the desire a perennial urge that keeps returning day after day and year after year, growing more colorful in its expression with each passing season. At this point, writing is more a blessing than it will ever be a curse—partly because I tentatively comprehend the mechanics of words, but mostly because I appreciate and understand the power of words.

There is a theory that exists within the context of conjectural African thought; it is the theory of Nomo: the power of the spoken word. In philosophical African reflection, words have a huge influence on how things are perceived and initiated. In his culturally celebrated book, *Muntu,* author Janheinz Jahn assert that awareness of this fact alone can reshape and alter our world. He goes on to explain: "That every human thought, once expressed, becomes reality" and that words not only initiates and sustain the course of things, but are also transformative. Because they have this power, "every word is an effective word" and "every word is binding." Within the notions of Nomo, there's no such thing as a "harmless, noncommittal word—every word has consequences. Therefore, the word binds the Muntu (man), and the Muntu is responsible for his word."

If I apply this concept to my writing, then every word that I type or scribble is useful in the context of the conversation I'm seeking to initiate. This is what we are all taught in English 101, to make our words count.

To remain honest to one's self and to reach across the chasm that separates us as people is no easy task. It seems every day we grow farther and farther apart as a species, and every moment we fall farther and farther from grace.

For me, words are too powerful and too precious to be given in complaint. I don't think we really understand how potent and complicated it is to speak and write them. If we did, then we would probably recognize that Hate is too harsh a word to use in reference to diets and exercise and TV shows we dislike—and especially towards people—and that Love is too prized a sentiment to be so casually attached to our favorite foods and movies.

As a writer I feel it is my calling to reveal the commonality that exists between us. Regardless of our preconceived differences, we have more in common with each other than with any other form of life on the planet, but what connects us to all salient life are our words and the meanings we attach to them.

So within the pages that follow are stories and bits and pieces of learning distilled from the stuff of my life experience, and that which I gleaned from others. What I discovered also was not just how much I loved writing, but how much I enjoyed sharing what I wrote—which in the end is the real reason writers write.

# Writing Out Loud

We make sense of our world by telling each other stories.
*-Carol Adrienne*

everal years ago, a close friend prompted me to start blogging on a popular social media site. I really wasn't that keen on the idea because, well, I have trust issues—especially when it comes to the internet and sharing my writing. And from what I had heard of blogging, it sounded kind of self-indulgent and narcissistic (not that I don't have the ego to support that type of behavior), and like everyone else, my day-to-day living was just about as exciting as that of a snail, and moved along at a similar pace.

**I** write because I feel I have something to say. And I learned that was the case with most people. It's lonely out there in the real world, and most of us are just trying to connect because we often feel so alienated and invisible. We want to be known, appreciated and valued because we have something to share whether it's mundane or profound.

**B**ut even more than that, blogging was a legitimate form of voyeurism in which one could engage without feeling embarrassed or sinful. Like a Peeping Tom looking between the vanes of a stranger's bedroom window—but in this case the stranger has knowingly drawn back the curtains and raised the blinds so that we might have an unrestricted view of their personal selves. It appeals to the child in us, and satisfies the deep desire and need to be both seen and heard; to add our voice to the chorus, to make sense of our world, as writer Carol Adrienne so perceptively puts it, "by telling each other stories." Blogging was where we put our
private selves on display for all the world to see and know. It was Writing Out Loud.

**A**s a writer, I realized that blogging was a phenomenal resource at this particular time in place—sure, the internet is mostly viewed as an innovative source for commerce and military exploitation, but its true value lies in its enormous ability to heighten the level of communication across the globe. Speaking before the National Press Club after the 2008 presidential election, former presidential candidate Howard Dean stated definitively that, "The internet is a community—it is a community of people who do not live in the same place." Nothing could be truer.

Having come to that realization, I thought, I can do this, but in a different and more meaningful way. So I chose not to write about the humdrum circumstance of my everyday life, but instead, to offer up short essays on my discovery of life. That woven between the many strands that attach the days to our lives are tiny revelations and accidental insights that help us make "sense of the world" in one way or another—all the "Aha" moments that pique our brain, but are rushed through so quickly that they seldom register as memory. This is what I wanted to write about and share—not so much in details of the particulars, but the discerning that came from each unfolding event and chance encounter that registered and helped shape the character of whom I was growing into being.

You would think, nearing sixty-two, that most of my growing and understanding would have been done by now, but to be honest, it can take one, possibly two lifetimes plus forever to understand the complexities of being human. Both knowing that and enjoying the discovery are more than half the fun.

In blogging, I rediscovered my boyhood self—you know, that person we all remember way back in the day before we gave away our truths, and sold our dreams to the highest bidder for pennies. If any one thing makes me more comfortable in my own skin these days, it is the reclaiming of those boyhood attributes, and the desire to let them mold and shape me into a better man, secure in a fresh, new understanding of himself.

I also discovered a vast universe of kindred spirits who reinforced my understanding that we are more alike than not alike. Some were simply housewives taking care of children while doing creative work on the side; others were social workers tirelessly working with underprivileged teenagers and battling the demoralizing effects of human trafficking. Struggling writers (like myself), and teachers and knitters and students studying abroad or at community colleges.

Some were mystics who practiced yoga and reiki; while others worked for non-profit community organizations. Men and women, straight and gay, artists, graphic designers, programmers, forklift operators, coffee house and home entrepreneurs, and self-proclaimed baby makers, and some just plain'ol food cookin' mamas sharing recipes and moments of enlightenment discovered while sifting flour.

Through blogging I rediscovered America. But it was an America seldom shared on the evening news. An America of people who actually loved their parents and family...of husbands and wives devoted to each other and to raising their children...of small business owners who cared about their hired workers. My America; diverse in marriages and partnerships, and always willing to share an encouraging word or respectfully offer a dissenting opinion.

What mattered was not what they did...but who they were...not what they had to say, but what they had to share—the butcher, the baker, the candlestick maker—everyday people—all of us trying to make sense of the world by telling each other stories.

I blogged no less that once a week (which was quite a bit for me, since I did have another life), but it helped me to write daily, which is the only way to become a better writer and grow more comfortable with the craft. It disciplined me in ways that are still relevant today.

# PART ONE
## Net Essays

‘But how can this be?
My teacher commands me: Press
ENTER to exit.”
-William Warriner

## New Beginnings

There are changes going on inside my life…and more importantly, inside of me. A slow and subtle shifting of consciousness set in motion by a string of seemingly unrelated events gently leading me back to myself.

This past summer has been interesting.

I began the year on a pretty positive note…having accomplished so much of what I had desired the previous year. I had finished the book and had laid out a vision of how I expected the year to go. But it's been said that we make plans and God laughs. To be honest, I don't mind the joke; I'm just glad he/she still has a sense of humor…and it was so much in full play this summer.

Living is a practice in learning. I know that sounds obvious and simplistic, but it's so easy not to be educated by our experiences. We're such contrary creatures, narcissistic and full of doubt. But that's the real beauty of being human…of being created, as Scripture likes to put it: "a little lower than the angels."

I like being human, and flawed, and full of doubt. It sets up the opportunity for me to be more, better, and confident that what I believe, think and do is on the right path; it took a long time for me to finally get that.

Life is journey, and journey is more than just travel. It's also about the unraveling of oneself…the dismantling of outdated ideas and habits; antiquated thinking and illusionary beliefs. Journey for me has been about the rediscovery of mystery, and I've learned that I'm all right with mystery, that I don't have to understand everything, and that everything doesn't have to have a reason. Sometimes things just are.

So, now I'm back to share with you—a sort of "how I spent my summer vacation," not so much in details of the particular, but in the essence of what is currently being distilled. I still have my sense of humor. It seems that Spirit and I make a pretty good comedic team…sort of like the Smothers Brothers on Grace. Anyway, I've hope your summer was as revealing as mine…look forward to sharing.

*What I've learned: When someone says "It's me, not you," they're probably right.*

# Reclaiming My Lost Self

It's funny, but most of who we think we are is often what other people expect us to be. What I mean is that, we might think we know who we are until it dawns on us that person is really not of our own design, but rather built from the parts of our trying to fulfill the expectation of others. Of course, within the context of all our relationships (as well as life in general), there will always be expectations. It's just that some are more legitimate than others.

Asking that someone change to meet our prospect of who we'd like them to be is a mistake that all too many of us make. We often do this from a place of our own lacking. The Jerry Maguire fallacy of "you complete me," which, if truth be told, is a very scary point of view. Two different halves never form a whole of anything, and in the case of relationships, only two whole people (separate and distinct in their completeness) can ever have a chance at forming something whole, new and truly unique.

The problem is: Being whole is really hard work, and it seems we loathe to do the hard work. We'd rather leave it to others or to God and fate; but there are things about ourselves that only we know and understand, so it becomes incumbent upon us to take responsibility for the person we want to be. Although others can have their input, the final discerning belongs to us, and us alone.

Those who influence us the most are often those who make little effort in trying to do so. They live their lives with a certain awareness, from a place of knowing, and it is the fruit of that living that we notice. How well a person's life works is directly related to what they believe, think and feel, and how congruent those ways are with the things they do and say.

Most of our lives work in jolts of stop and go. But it is possible for it to be more harmonious, to not be constantly living on the edge—afraid to answer the phone or open the mail; discouraged by the things we have to do and the people who inhabit the landscape of our lives.

I feel blessed because most of my life works. That's not to say that everything is perfect; I would have loved to have gotten married and had a daughter, but that didn't happen. My life, however, is filled with the joy of a few good friends, and what I currently do for a living sustains me both financially and internally. I have a number of creative passions that fill my days with unfettered satisfaction and, I like to think, add something positive to the world.

All of this came about because I could no longer afford or allow who I was to be hidden under the expectations—no, scratch that— but rather the "wants" of others. To that end, I began the fight of reclaiming my lost spirit. It took a long time to finally get to this place, but believe me, it was a battle well worth waging.

## Rediscovering Mystery

It's easy to fall into the habit of just living, especially if you're single. But it can happen also if you're married, with children or a significant other. Life becomes a routine of events strung together by the dictates of the situation we've created for ourselves. Sometimes by choice, most times by accident.

We live in such small worlds. Surrounded by the people we know; the music we like, the opinions that suit our frame of reference. Stepping outside of our comfort zone is hard since we will be challenged by the diversity of a larger world: people who do not look like us, music unfamiliar in syncopation and sound, opinions that confront the very fabric of our own often narrow point of view. Life can lose a lot of its meaning in the comfort of the familiar. So once again I am challenged by mystery.

When I open myself to the larger world, I become larger. When I expose myself to different people and opinions and perspectives, I expand my capacity to understand while suspending judgment (since it's impossible to judge or have an opinion about things I really don't know). Case in point: when I consider the essence of homosexuality, I have to admit that I am totally hetero (I really love women). I can't even begin to understand loving a member of my gender with the same intensity as that which I feel for members of the opposite sex—but there are people who do.

I can say that it's not normal, but normal is subjective. I can say that it's not natural, but since nature is said to "abhor a vacuum," I must assume that there is something that somehow needs to be fulfilled (neither am I that arrogant or mean as to declare to my gay friends that what they experience is unnatural). In short, I am left with mystery; the simple fact that I just don't understand. And I'm all right with that. The same can be said of God and Republicans (just kidding). There are things and ways of being that simply elude me. And that's okay. I don't know everything and neither do I feel the need to. Understanding this has freed me up from trying to convince others that they are wrong—which doesn't mean I never challenge an opposing opinion; simply that I am not invested in doing so.

As I become more cognizant of living, I have begun to notice that most of my life is ruled by mystery. They are the things that I assume about other people, the actions that can't be explained, the feelings I have for no reasons other than what I intuit. I am humbled by this place of unknowing. Mystery, for me, is forgiveness for being flawed and human. It is Spirit at his/her most loving.

## Starting Points

I'm a big believer in starting points. You know, like New Year's Eve and birthdays. I used to put things off just to have them as jumping-off places to begin something new and different in improving the quality of my life. What I eventually learned was that any time can be a starting point, and, to be honest, no time is really better than the present.

Every morning we wake up, every breath we've been blessed to take, every hour, minute, second, is an opportunity to start over and begin again. Like forgiving a past wrong or keeping a promise, few things are as valuable as the opportunity we have now, in this moment, to be more…to be better.

We take a lot for granted. We think tomorrow is promised to us and so we spend an awful lot of time doing things we don't want to do...believing things we don't really believe in. We waste an awful lot of time being contrary about things that really don't matter.

I'm tired of doing that. I've already had the fearful childhood, the lonely adolescence, and the bitter uncertainty of early adulthood. The thirties brought about an inkling of understanding that there was something more to be had from living other than sex, money and career.

The forties were a subtle clearing of the fog and an appreciation of the fact that I actually survived. And the fifties, well, the fifties became a declaration of independence on nearly every level one can imagine. Nobody, really, nobody wears life like the person who has lived to be fifty. At fifty you wear life like Saturday clothes.

I want more, and a truer meaning for the circumstance of my life—my first commitment being to myself for the kind of person that Spirit wants me to be.

There is a favorite line from the movie *The Russia House*, where Sean Connery says to Michelle Pfeiffer: "All my failings were preparations for meeting you." That is the essence of who I want to be. I want to be that man who has grown from all the things that he has failed at being, all the mistakes he unintentionally made.

It takes a lifetime to come to grips with who we are. I've lived and continue to live that lifetime. I know who I am. I'm the best me that I've ever been—and I'm not through yet.

Still. I'm a big believer in starting points....and running starts...and new beginnings. As another year rapidly comes to a close, I make this promise to myself and to the Spirit that watches over me that I will not approach this new year in the same manner as the last. I will speak more honestly and be more supportive of all that's good to go in this troubled world.

I will cry more openly and laugh more loudly. Regardless of all that has happened in the past, I will continue to remain open to the act of loving.

Starting here and now...alone on this planet circling the sun.

# Saturday Clothes

We come into this world afraid of letting go, and continue this process up until the moment we are forced to do so for the very last time. But life is all about starting over and letting go; birthing dreams and watching them grow. Some are aborted early, others abandoned later; most might even mature enough to see the light of day. But it's sort of like playing the lottery: You can't win if you never buy a ticket.

There are some guarantees in life; they're just not the ones we want. It's pretty much guaranteed that if you open your heart to love, you will be hurt; and that people regardless of their intention will undoubtedly disappoint you. You're guaranteed to be misunderstood often, and to fail more times than not. But letting go and living, I mean really living, improves the stakes and increases the odds that you will love passionately, have friendships that last a lifetime, and grow and succeed beyond your wildest imaginings.

Sometime we hold onto too much—not just children and old clothes that no longer fit, but old and antiquated ways of thinking and believing. For sure there is comfort in ritual and the status quo, but there is also the danger of being out of step and left behind, simply because life is not static. It's full of uncertainty, mystery and joy and is always, always in flux.

It's good to develop a philosophy about living; a way of engaging the world beyond our fears and failings. I used to think the more I enjoyed life, the harder it would be to someday surrender it. I think now that it is actually the opposite: The more passionately I embrace living—whether by chance or circumstance—the more satisfied I will be at the end of my days.

I want to wear my life like Saturday clothes. You know, like that favorite pair of jeans that fits so well in all the right places and compliments your behind. Carefully picked over and viewed in the dressing room mirror, then worn home from the store because they looked and felt so good that you couldn't bear to take them off. Washed on gentle cycles and saved for special occasions where they were sure to draw a compliment.

Then one day, while doing laundry, they're splattered with bleach, snagged at the pocket or stained while mowing the grass. You feel that sudden twinge of regret, of loss, but letting go is just the beginning, as you relegate them to Saturdays, where they continue to get broken in with house repairs and gardening, cleaning out the garage, being spit up on while babysitting the neighbor's kid. They grow loose and shabby and faded; torn at the knees and frayed at the cuffs but still hold their form and flatter your behind.

You find yourself coming home from work or a party, and hurriedly pitching the business attire or little black dress for the comfort of those tattered jeans. Climbing into them is like climbing into the arms of a well-worn lover, who knows your body and smells of Cheer and Downy softener and the sweetness of having just showered. Saturday clothes…lived in and worn well.

## Living at the speed of now

He fell in love the first moment he laid eyes on her; on the second day after she moved into the house across the street from where he lived. At eleven, and every bit a boy up until that point; she awakened a sleeping desire that rivaled his worship of comic book heroes and fishing, and the warm feeling he felt from his father's shoulder hug.

Fast friends from the start, they fell easily into hanging out; climbing trees and chasing crayfish in the clear, deep waters of the creek behind his house. They shared grade school classes and neighborhood birthday parties, and the only awkward moment he could ever recall was a time while hiking together in the woods outside of town, he glimpsed her peeing.

She was squatting—jeans shoved to the ground, arms hooked about her knees. She met his eyes as she slowly drew herself erect, her soft, cotton panties gently caressing her lithe, reddish brown thighs as she pulled them up to cover the tiny fluff of hair nested between her legs. Unabashed, she simply smiled as if to say, "Someday...someday I will be yours."

She moved away at thirteen, but promised to write him every week, and made a pact that should they ever find themselves alone in life, to seek the other out. But as the weeks turned into months, her letters never came and so he moved on, and grew up, and thought of her, then married, and moved away, and had children, and thought of her and came back and buried his father, and later divorced—always wondering whatever became of her, his first love.

And recalling their pact, he set about searching for her on MySpace and Facebook only to discover that she had died in an accident two weeks after moving away, back when she was only thirteen.

So why am I telling you this story? I'm telling you this story because life is not a promised gift. I'm telling you this because late one night while I was out running errands, singer Michael Jackson died, and earlier that same week, actress and poster girl Farrah Fawcett—and hidden away in the daily paper, flanked by an advertisement announcing the latest pre-winter sale, was a small article about an eight-year-old girl who lost her two-year battle with cancer. Life is not a promised gift for any of us. It doesn't matter how famous or how old or how rich or how unique we think we are.

Life is lived at the speed of now; whatever we put off today may never happen, and whoever doesn't know that we love them today may never know tomorrow. Life happens...but living is something altogether different. It is an understanding and awareness that in any moment things can change for the better as well as for the worst, and that it is up to us to make the most of this particular time in place.

We live in fast and furious times, often bordered by despair and loss on one side, and hope and prosperity on the other—there are no guarantees. But providence has given us favor and implores us to live our best life now.

# Standing in Grace

A good friend recently told me in so many words that she was put off by my "relentless happiness." Of course, I took issue with the word relentless, which seems to exemplify a type of bullying constancy. I also took issue with the word happiness coupled with relentless—it offered up this image of some enlightened idiot overflowing with good cheer.

In my own defense, I have to confess to a constancy in attitude. It's not like I don't have my moments of frustration, disappointment and utter despair. I do. However, they are just that, moments; they're not the entire day or, for that matter, not even the next moment following.

I attribute a lot of this to Grace…those small moments of forgiveness that shelter us from catastrophe and make us exclaim, "OMG." Our lives are replete with examples that go unheralded every day. They are the calamities that are avoided for reasons we will never understand; the disasters that are sidestepped by a second's hesitation or a decision made in an instant that changes our lives forever.

I once took a trip to South Dakota to visit a new friend—a 500-mile trek across two borders that took nearly nine hours of driving. It was a journey along highways under constant construction…cruising for miles down roads that alternated between two- and single-lane traffic. It rained off and on and detours were common, and following single file became the norm—and, of course, the conditions were the same on the way back.

The next day, after arriving back home, I was out and about doing errands when my car started to lose power. I was about a half-mile away from my mechanic's shop and was just barely able to get there before the brakes locked up. Later, I got a call from my mechanic saying that he didn't know what had gone wrong with the brakes, but that the drums had gotten so hot they had turned blue. He said that it was gonna cost at least $500 just to find out what the problem was.

Now, one might think, what an unfortunate event and expense, but it could have been worse. Just imagine if serendipity had not been present; then somewhere, 500 miles away from home in the middle of nowhere on a one-lane construction highway, I could have broken down, or even worse…caused an accident. It helped me to understand that the things which happen in our lives are neither good nor bad; they are simply the things that happen in our lives. We give them meaning by how we choose to interpret them.

Our lives are lived in increments of the now. It took a long time for me to come to that understanding, but once I did, I realized that how I choose to feel in any given situation is incumbent upon how I choose to be in that moment or in the moments following. Most of the time I'm simply standing in grace...blessed with the understanding that I choose joy.

Now that makes me "relentlessly happy."

## Everyday Sacred

Several Sundays back I spent the morning and early afternoon with a dear friend. We met a little over ten years ago when I was in my early forties and on the rebound from a failed engagement. Originally from England, she was in her mid-fifties, her husband having died several years earlier. She was a big part of a healing process that would change me forever and was instrumental in the writing of my first book.

The plan was for me to drive up and she would prepare breakfast; then we would catch an early movie: *Julie and Julia*. The conversation is always good and usually covers a variety of subjects—from politics and the latest books to what's currently going on in our lives.

Breakfast, as always, is a simple, exquisite treat. This time it was BLTs, built upon a soft, circular and gently seasoned flatbread, with delicately crisp strips of bacon bedded on green lettuce and thinly sliced garden tomatoes; a light smear of mayo, topped with a generous tablespoon of fresh salsa with just the slightest hint of sweetness; sliced cantaloupe and blueberries with a glass of OJ and stoutly brewed coffee on the side—the presentation convivial in its old-world simplicity.

The movie turned out to be the perfect complement to the morning. Meryl Streep's deft portrayal of the late Julia Child was right on, and suggestive of how my English friend approaches living.

There's a simple joy in everything she does; from sewing to cooking to tending her yard and garden. Walking with her in the woods behind her house or along paved trail walkways is never simply a hike or a stroll, but rather an adventure in appreciation of the natural world, an elevation of the common into something to be fully indulged, experienced and enjoyed, and dare I add, very English.

It's hard to describe her enjoyment of the ordinary. She'll say to me, "Come, look at this flower." And gently tilt the sleepy bloom, carefully revealing its dazzling swirls of color in a cascade of light. Or, "Taste this," as she pinches off a piece of some new bread she found at the corner market, delighting in the texture of its taste.

She reminds me that life is savored in a thousand different ways…in the small ways the usual is shown to grace our days. Driving away from visiting her, I find myself renewed. In the moments afterward, I am replete with the realization that this is what I crave most from living: an awareness of all the little moments in the life I have—and in the life that has me.

## The Power of No

*"No! It's a complete sentence."-Anne Lamott*

Saying No is one of the hardest things to do when it comes to other people, yet one of the easiest things to do when it comes to denying ourselves. For a long time, self-denial was a problem that mostly afflicted women, but it's just as much a problem for men—why else do you think they've become workaholic husbands and absentee fathers?

Both Yes and No are very definitive statements; they help redefine us in a thousand small ways that we never knew existed. There are no gray areas in such a declaration, and for good reasons. In today's conflicted society, where people like politicians flip-flop as easy as flapjacks at a breakfast buffet, such waffling can lead to a lot of misunderstandings and distress. But, when we say No, clearly, definitively, we leave little doubt about the meaning of our discourse or obscuring our intention, thereby making it much easier for us to be heard.

If most of who we think we are is what other people expect us to be, then saying No begins to rectify that by bringing who we are into clearer focus—with ourselves as well as with others. With a clearer understanding of who we are and what we say, we can begin to fashion a new vision for ourselves; one that challenges all our outmoded thinking about what it really means to be present in every aspect of our lives.

That saying No implies an opposing response is somewhat ironic. In declining one thing, we are opting for another. We are saying Yes in regards to the important relationships in our lives and to the things that matter most. When we embrace No as a mantra, we honor the power of words and bring a forgotten sacredness to the discriminating use of language. As therapist and writer Deena Metzger notes in the opening chapter of her book *Writing for Your Life*: "The world of public discourse—political, social, diplomatic, commercial—has so corrupted language that we are rightly more suspicious of the meaning of words than we are convinced of their veracity."

I agree. Saying No is a very liberating thing. It frees us up to pursue activities that really matter on both a personal and professional level. But even more important, saying No makes it possible for us to say Yes to life in a way that is more harmonious and beneficial. If No is a complete sentence, as Anne Lamott so astutely discerned, then Yes is a complete affirmation—and affirming what we believe to be a fundamental truth about ourselves is highly instrumental in stimulating the changes necessary in moving us forward into a different kind of life.

In the end, No is more than just a complete sentence. It's the first word in the beginning of a new conversation with ourselves.

## Saying Yes

If saying No is the first word in the beginning of a new conversation with ourselves, then saying Yes is our continuing dialogue with the larger world. To the extent that No puts a stop to all the things that we really don't want to do, saying yes opens the door to the myriad beginning that living has to offer.

When we say Yes to life, we begin an exploration not only of ourselves, but of others, and all that's involved in living a more authentic life. Yes opens us up to new possibilities. It is the go button...our "get out of jail free" card, allowing us to embrace life more spontaneously.

# What I know (part one)

Women have always informed my life—in literature (Maya Angelou, Gloria Steinem), in music (Joni Mitchell, Mary J. Blige), but seldom in relationships. I think that's because most of my relationships have been with women damaged by the vulgarities of the people in their lives. Whether through the dictates of parents, or sibling rivalries; or surviving the abuse of failed relationships and marriages…in some huge way something traumatized them, making it extremely difficult for them to have the kinds of supportive relationships that so many of us desire.

I think this is also true of men, and probably of people in general. We seldom learn from the wounded…and neither can the wounded learn from us. For some, overcoming the hurts of the past is a constant challenge and, if not confronted early, influences the outcome of most of their interactions with others.

For those who choose to do the hard work of working through those ghosts that haunt the dark corridors of their psyche, things do get better. But like I've expressed so many times before, doing the hard work, well, is hard work. And sometimes we're just not up for it.

It's so hard to be objective when it comes to analyzing our own behavior and neurosis. All of us like to think that it's "them" not "us," but the truth probably rests somewhere in the middle (usually, a little bit of them and a lot of us). I guess that's why it's more important for me to know who I am, rather than to be right. If I know who I am, then when I'm wrong, I become enlightened—which only can lead to a better me, and being a better me is what I believe my life is really all about.

There's an old saying: "If you don't stand for something, you'll fall for anything." But I think it also depends on the something that you stand for. For some people, anything will do. Most of us don't know enough about who we are, and so we're always stumbling into situations that challenge what we think and believe and often find ourselves lacking. We martyr our dreams for the benefit of parents and sell our souls to jobs we don't enjoy. We shamelessly give in to our children and to the dictates of relatives and would-be friends or ideologically opposed pundits.

We've become so disillusioned, that we're willing to believe in anything but ourselves. So we latch onto both fact and fantasy in support of all the things we doubt, and fear, and don't know. We fill the mystery in our lives with myth and fallacy, and a personalized truth that makes us comfortable and safe.

This is what I know of myself—this is what I know about being human.

# Luck

It's been said that life is lived forward, but experienced backward. So it seems if we're fortunate we get two chances at living. Our first chance comes from a place of not knowing—from experiencing, and our second from a place of understanding—from having experienced.

These chances at a second go-round usually start somewhere around middle age and are all about being whole and comfortable in our own skin. It's about developing a philosophy in regards to living, a way of engaging the world beyond our fears and failings. It's recognizing that the more passionately we embrace life, whether by accident or fate, the more satisfied we'll be at the end of the day when death comes knocking at the door.

Being whole is hard work, and at times, we loathe to do the hard work. We'd rather leave it to others or to God and luck, but there are things about ourselves that only we know and understand; so it becomes incumbent upon us to take responsibility for the things we want to happen. And even though others can have their input, the final discerning belongs to us and us alone. Those who influence us the most are usually those who make little effort in trying to do so. We call them the "lucky ones." They live their lives with a keen sense of awareness, from a place of knowing. And how well their life works is directly related to what they believe, think and feel, and how congruent those ways are with the things they do and say.

In his book *The Luck Factor*, scientist Richard Wiseman contends that there are four defining attributes of people who consider themselves lucky: maximizing their chance opportunities; listening to their intuition; expecting the best; and lastly, their ability to turn unfortunate circumstance into good. These attributes, he determined, lay at the heart of why circumstance seemed always to favor them.

Casting aside the notions of amulets and lucky charms, and daring to shatter mirrors while walking under ladders, Dr. Wiseman, through thoughtful analysis and scientific testing, challenges the mysticism connected to good fortune.

His final conclusion? It's "personality" that makes the biggest difference; that, comparatively speaking, both lucky and unlucky people had the same odds at randomly winning the lottery, but "lucky people's expectations of winning were more than twice that of unlucky people." And it is our expectations that make the difference in how we grapple with the vulgarities of day-to-day living.

Albert Einstein made a similar summation. When queried what he considers to be one of the most instructive questions one could ask of himself, his reply was whether one believed "the universe was a friendly place." The belief and expectation that the universe is a friendly place plays a major part in our actions and how we respond to the various circumstances of living. In a world full of random acts and happenstance, not to believe so often leaves one at a huge disadvantage.

Lucky people believe in themselves and the world around them. Left in an awful situation through no fault of their own, they make the assumption that things could always be worse, look for ways to improve their lot, trust their instincts, envision the best and move on. For them luck is simply a state of mind, and a way of being in the world that embraces optimism and change, and a vague assurance that the universe is on their side—and is, indeed, a friendly place.

## Having Attitude

There is a scene from a little-known movie titled *Phoebe in Wonderland*, where a grade-school drama teacher says to a troubled student, "At a certain point in your life—probably when too much of it has gone by—you will open your eyes and see yourself for who you are...especially for everything that made you so different from all the awful normals. And you will say to yourself: but 'I am this person,' and in that statement, that correction, there will be a kind of love." The "kind of love" she is referring to, is the kind that we only can give from what we know about who we are and who we mean to be. This is in direct correlation to the attitude we have about ourselves as a person individually distinct from others.

In the neighborhood where I grew up, if you were a proud child raised with a good heart and a strong sense of self, it showed in your stature and the way you walked. The old folks setting out on their front porches late in the evening watching the young people strut, called it "having attitude" as opposed to "having an attitude." And even though you might think the distinction strictly semantics, it's much more than that.

"Having attitude" is something you possess; "having an attitude" is something that possesses you. Having attitude was displayed in the way Michael Jordan played basketball, and in the way Muhammad Ali retained the title. It's a look and a way of inhabiting your place on the planet that says: I know who I am, and it matters.

Having attitude is crucial to your own personal sense of worth; in how much you are willing to trust yourself and your own judgments and perceptions. It's what you bring to the table that will distinguish you from "*all the awful normals.*" Few things are as debilitating as not being able to trust our own opinion or truth about a thing regardless of what others might be telling us.

Too many of us grow up with "an attitude." We wear it prominently, like a chip on the shoulder just waiting for someone to knock it off—and set us off. Having an attitude usually comes from a strong sense of entitlement; the belief that the world owes us something simply by virtue of who we are, and where we come from. It's hubris in its most insidious form. And it's capable of wreaking havoc not only on the lives of those in passing, but also in the lives of those closest to us and eventually on ourselves; because having an attitude is what we lay on the table in defiance to all other differences and opinions—in disregard to the feelings of others and in objection to the commonsensical and sane. It's where all the "awful normals" hide and justify the cruel and appalling things they do that continues to make the world an unsafe place.

There is a saying: "*Everyone is born unique...but most of us die copies.*" We copy the lies and truth of our families, the joys and betrayals of our lovers, the envy and devotions of our friends and relatives and the myriad people who traverse the landscape of our lives. But we were meant to be more than just copies. We were meant to be co-creators in a universe waiting to rejoice in the magnitude of who we are. We were not meant to settle for less out of fear, shame or any misguided sense of responsibility. We were meant to be great, and lead extraordinary lives.

## Joy

I've heard it said that there is no such thing as "blind faith"—that fundamentally faith is "visionary." Christian scripture aptly describes it as "the substance of things hoped for...evidence of things not seen" (Hebrews). Those same scriptures also say, "for lack of a vision the people perish," so it would seem the two are somewhat linked together. If faith is truly visionary, then it should come as no surprise that those who get what they want out of life are those who are capable of seeing as well as believing in the possibility of their dreams.

Most of us know that the phrase "the pursuit of happiness" is one of the defining lines written by Thomas Jefferson in the first paragraph of the *Constitution*. Along with life and liberty, Jefferson rightfully assumed that all three were necessary components in the construction of a free society.

However, the pursuit of happiness has long been the leading cause for much of the consternation we experience in life. Like most things external, happiness is transitory and dependent upon the outcome of a particular situation. It's often short-lived and fleeting, lasting only as long as the moment's experience.

There is, however, an elusive experience whose shelf life is nearly inexhaustible—one frequently confused with happiness because of its similar attributes, but derived from an entirely different prospective. This is the experience of Joy.

Joy exists as a state of being. And even though it too can be a momentary flash, its afterglow can last forever because it originates from our awareness and appreciation that every moment is simply just that. It is the result of internal feelings of good will linked to our thankfulness for just being alive.

Joy takes those moments of happiness and deepens them. Most of us have known this feeling at one time or another but have failed to recognize it for what it was: in a sky ablaze with the blush of a setting sun; in the hush of a child suckling sleep in its mother's arms; in the sweet, soft scent of a lover lying next to us in a darkness broken only by the whispering movement of a smile. We have known such small moments to be full of serenity and the awareness that life is good even if our current circumstance is not.

In an e-mail interview author Elizabeth Gilbert, in referencing her book *Eat, Pray, Love*, expressed a similar belief concerning crisis and adversity and its connection to the holy: *"I don't believe that suffering is the only path to the divine. Epic instances of joy and overwhelming waves of happiness also bring us to the brink of transcendence. At either extreme, God is waiting. It's only in the mundane that we sort of lose our ability to experience wonder and miracles."* (Italics mine) I agree. However, I also would reason that the mundane becomes extraordinary through those "epic instances of joy," which, though brief, still transcend most moments of happiness. The difference lies in the quality of those moments and how it relates to a feeling of satisfaction.

Joy is the essence of living done right. It is what I believe God felt after the hard work of creation, when he took a moment out from playing with clay to say to himself, *"This is good."*

## Living at Your Own Pace

In a tattered storage box filled with loose newspaper articles and clippings is the obituary of an attractive, successful, fifty-two-year-old woman. It seems she caught a bad case of the flu and was having a hard time shaking it off. So she went to her doctor, and they ran a few tests and unexpectedly discovered that she had a massive brain tumor and was expected to live only a couple of weeks.

Another one hits the high points in the life of a thirty-five-year-old man, an athlete and avid cyclist who, while out on a weekend ride with friends, slumped over his bike and never regained consciousness.

Both accounts are ominous testimonials to the fact that when it comes right down to it, we really don't know anything about what is actually going on inside our body or, for all that matters, outside the realm of any of our five natural senses.

We take so much for granted these days, especially this reward called life. We repeatedly put off living with all our favorite curt and clichéd sayings such as: "I'll do it tomorrow," or "I'll have more time when the kids are grown." But the reality is there are no guarantees. Life happens, and it's happening now even as I type these words.

Deep inside the firma of our body, a plethora of incredible things is going on. Blood rushing along arterial highways shares the road with plaque and other genetic anomalies left unchecked by diet and exercise. Our brain, under pressure from living at a hectic pace, pounds from exhaustion and our hearts break under the constant strain of failed relationships and marriages. Our feet hurt and our bowels back up. We toss and turn restlessly, caught up in a darkness filled with the anguish of disquieting dreams. We are forever at odds with life and what it all might mean.

Then one morning, we awaken with a slight pain in the chest or a hint of indigestion. We shower, having ignored the small lump beneath our breast or the scaly eruption of skin that hasn't healed. We drive to work oblivious to the fact that our head hurts and our body aches for reasons we would rather not know, until we're suddenly saddled with a heart attack or invaded with a prognosis of cancer or HIV.

Life happens, and we are constantly assaulted by the speed at which it does. Surrounded by war and disease, poverty, greed and incivility, it's no wonder we want to pass through with blinders on, arrogant in the belief that living is somehow locked in. Yet in the eyes of providence we are neither special nor ordinary but only slightly blessed for having been created *"a little lower than the angels."*

The reason we feel the way we do is because we're so dissatisfied and constantly reacting to the way life has been laid out for us. Trapped between the minimalisms of yesterday and the convolutions of today, we yield to the busyness of living, multitasking ourselves into distraction; buying into a cynicism that infects our attitude like a virulent disease, eating away at our dreams and heart's desires and killing our faith like a self-fulfilling prophecy. But it only feels that way because we're not doing what we really want and being who we really are. And the only real way to counter that belief is to slow down and start living at our own pace.

Living at our own pace acknowledges the fact that life is about this moment; that simplicity in living and doing makes it possible to separate what is truly important from that which we have been marketed to believe in. If we are hurried and preoccupied with multitasking, we become acclimated to that lifestyle and eventually miss out on all those small moments that give us respite from a world which relentlessly grinds away at our spirit. Recent research has shown that when we multitask, the quality of each task is diminished and we actually don't accomplish as much as we think we do.

When life is approached from the perspective of this moment, we slow down and begin to respect the significance as well as the insignificance of our place in the grand scheme of things. Understanding how insignificant we really are in comparison to the larger issues of the world brings immediate significance to the abuse of our time on the planet.

Living at our own pace is not so much about challenging today's current reality as it is about working our lives around it by being present. We seem to want to do it all, but seldom give ourselves enough time in which to do it all. Living at our own pace settles that problem by placing our awareness at the center of not needing to feel rushed. And we accomplish this by giving everything we do its proper due in attention and time.

In this world of instant gratification, it's easy to find ourselves at odds with time and circumstance. Our modern demands are so many: kids, work, shopping, continuing adult education—and that's just the good stuff. Divorce, unemployment, bad healthcare options, and the occasional financial misstep, snip at our heels like celebrity dogs gone wild.

But, we actually know how much time it takes to commute to work, cook, feed the kids and assist them with their homework. We know the time it takes to pay the monthly bills or shop for this week's groceries. It's that regardless of our knowing, we still try to squeeze just one thing more into the mix so that we usually end up late or hurried.

Living at our own pace is easiest when we're about doing what we really want to be doing with our life. We spend a lot of time chasing after dreams that bring us little joy, and for all the wrong reasons. We pursue profession based upon the dictates of our parents and develop friendships tailored to the opinions of small- minded relatives or class-conscious co-workers. And like fattened calves we willfully follow after the marketing of the larger society as it gleefully leads us off to financial slaughter.

We think it chic to waste an awful amount of time learning from our own mistakes, simply ignoring the past experiences of those who came before us. We do these things out of habit and a casual distrust of our own intuition, but mostly, we do it out of a misguided notion that we have an infinite amount of time at our disposal.

The truth is this: Every time we put something off, every time we disavow a dream, we run the risk of losing out on all that living has to offer us in fulfilling our destiny. It's been said that the wealthiest place on earth can be found in the graveyards of every town and country across the planet. For beneath those marbled headstones and bone-gray markers lie inventions that were never made, equations that were never formulated, and myriad loves left unrequited...simply because they were never chanced. If there are elements of living that assault our psyche, this has got to be the gravest of them all: to live a life of unfulfilled aspiration.

When we embrace this Now moment, we embrace the possibilities of every dream we can ever conceive. When we embrace this Now moment, we embrace life.

## What I know (part two)

We were meant to stand for more than just something...and to be more than just anything. It's been said that, to be born a human being, instead of a snake, is a wonderful opportunity; so whether we know it or not, we are obligated simply by the unique nature of our being to be more. And we can be.

We start out like everybody else with our likes and dislikes—and we are very upfront and straightforward about them; we trust both ourselves and others to do and be who they say they are. During this childhood, the most honest season of our lives, the nascent defining of ourselves has little to do with outside labels and everything to do with who we are—deep down in our soul, where the spirit is always young and self-affirming.

It's our innocence that gives us this extraordinary ability to see the world in a brighter light, but as we grow older, we encounter the ills and foibles of the larger society; we become jaded and our sense of wonder stunted. On the doorsteps of adolescence we bear the weight of an awareness that is indicative of our coming of age—the loss of our innocence and, along with it, our emerging sense of self.

Understanding this is crucial in the resurrection of our childhood spirit. Acknowledging that we had surrendered, at some point, to the assault on our psyche by those who both love and loathe us in our efforts to be more, is the hardest confession we will ever make, but one that we must make if we are ever to live up to our individual potential. The truth is simple: We become what we believe...and what we believe in and about ourselves is the substratum on which we will build the indelible character of our person.

Who am I…is more than just a question I ask myself. It is a question that will be asked of me over and over again by the world at large, and in every challenging situation I might encounter. How I answer will depend on what I believe and know to be true about myself and what I stand for— deep down in my soul, where the spirit is always young and self-affirming.

So what do I believe?

I believe that being human is a privilege and a gift; with a sense of self and purpose that acknowledges its imperfection while striving to be more.

I believe that honesty, if not the best, is a pretty good policy; that people who don't blame others for their personal despairs are probably more fair-minded; and that those who make no excuses for their failures usually win in the end.

I believe in group affliction and individual triumphs; that there was a Holocaust, a Middle Passage, a Trail of Tears. I believe we are all prophets in the fulfillment of our own destinies and that we can always be better than our faulted histories.

I believe that age is but a number, and that black, white, rich, poor, liberal and conservative are simply generalizations that separate us from one another and make impossible the peace of the world.

I believe, regardless of the evening news, that the world is a benevolent place, that people are basically good, that crime doesn't pay, and that what we put out into the universe returns in kind.

I believe in friends to die for, parents to care for and elders to respect; that the abandoned child, the abused woman, the homeless man and the wounded soldier are all my responsibility—and that I am indeed my brother's keeper.

I believe in sexual orientation and the love between two people, regardless of gender. I believe in monogamy and the joys of an exclusive relationship. I believe that loving someone, anyone, is never a sacrifice, and that words said in anger are seldom forgotten.

I believe that men are physically stronger than women—but that doesn't make women any weaker—and that women are emotionally more resilient than men—but that doesn't make men any less feeling.

I believe the body is a temple designed to lengthen and enhance our time on the planet, and that choosing to abuse it with unhealthy habits is a desecration that is not readily forgiven.

I believe in making bread from scratch, chopping vegetables by hand, and that supplements can be a poor excuse for not eating better. I believe in laughter, giving gifts for no reason, long hugs and deep kisses; the mending of broken hearts and the forgiving of trespasses.

I believe in fast starts, slow goes and final finishes; that life is good and filled with a lot of incredible, edifying moments.

I believe in simplicity.

I believe in a past for reflection, a tomorrow full of promise and a today for being present; that the memory of yesterday is always sweeter than today; and that each generation thinks that it's more blessed than the one which came before.

I believe in the worth of all living things and that the earth is a sanctuary to which we were given the privilege of its stewardship. I believe that the changing of the seasons is a cleansing of our destructive ways and that there will be an ending.

I believe in a Spirit that is constant and kind, and munificent in helping me to make sense of my place on the planet…and that its essence is a deep and enduring affection. I believe that scripture is the errant interpretation of men and that its power lies in the poetry of its intent to enlighten and inspire. I believe that miracles happen after a lot of hard work and that God is not only in the details, but in all the elements left out and in between. And I believe in faith, hope and charity, and that the greatest of these is love.

I believe that this list can go on forever—and that knowing the specific of these things informs my life, sustains my character and gives authority to the things I do and say. They have nothing to do with being right, only what I have discerned to be right for myself in an attempt to stand my ground, and not be batted about willy-nilly. To take arms, to paraphrase Shakespeare…against a storm of disparate judgments, and by opposing them…end them.

This is what I know about myself. This is what I know about being human.

# PART TWO
## All About Love

"I live with the beauty of regret, and the memory of love."
-Diane Keaton

# Falling in Love

In the 1980's romantic comedy *He Said She Said*, Elizabeth Perkins and Kevin Bacon portray television personalities with opposing points of view who also happen to be living together. In the middle of an argument (based upon that historical relationship question: Where is this heading?), she finally asks him if he ever thinks about marriage. "Sure," he answers earnestly. "I think about marriage—I just don't know what I think about it."

For most of us, falling in love is easy; it's committing to something more lasting that's difficult. To be honest, as a confirmed bachelor and head cheerleader for male "quirky-aloneness," I'm probably the last person to be offering his opinion on the matter. But then again, who better?

I was the consummate romantic; raised on all the right movies and quixotic fantasies of love and chivalry. Not that there was anything wrong with that, other than the fact that it was totally unrealistic and set me up for a roller coaster ride of disappointment. Most movies and romance novels are simply exaggerated examples of how we spend our time on the planet. In them, we come off appearing far more noble, caring and honest than we actually are in real life while, at the same time, just as equally nefarious, selfish and manipulative than most of us can possibly ever be. At least I like to think so. Still, nothing in the annals of human development has done more damage to our collective consciousness than our distorted perceptions of romantic love.

A good friend of mine likes to use a cooking metaphor in describing relationships. He says most couplings heat up quickly and then go into a rapid boil depending on how high they turn up the heat. At this point, he explains, we just throw in all the good stuff, reserving nothing. We tell everything and have sex way too soon, when we should be slow-cooking it, adding a little spice here and there, and keeping some of the family seasoning a mystery.

I would be remiss if I didn't confess to the truth of his comments. Pushed by the technology that drives our lives, we seem to rush pell-mell into every aspect of living; multitasking our time away with emails and smart phones and iPods and the latest gadget that goes beep in the dark.

We speed-date and join online match sites searching for that proverbial "soul mate," our "other half"...the one who "gets us"...that ultimate connection leading up to our own personal "Jerry McGuire" moment of completion.

My friend tells me that the best relationships are like homemade chili, put together slowly from scratch, and just gets better with each passing day. Every time it's heated up, the ingredients blend and meld and flavor themselves into the unique dish that it was meant to become. It's not a prepackaged thing; neither does it need to be supersized or garnished with the salty opinions of others. We know what tastes good.

Still, how something tastes is not always the best indication of how healthy it will be for us. Some relationships feel good but leave a bad taste in our mouths right after the first kiss. And like most things with specialized appeal, we tend to overindulge in them and then ignore the symptoms of things that don't seem to settle right. Like undercooked pork or a bad burrito takeout from the night before, we have an inkling of wrong; a vague churning in the gut followed by a burp of flatulence signaling there's something awful stinky in Denmark.

Our intuition tells us that we're allergic to this particular type of behavior, but we go wheezing and coughing onto the next date, our eyes and nose red from the first symptoms of emotional and mental abuse. We forgive him for not showing up or calling; we let slide the fact that she bounces checks. We overlook the lies uncovered, the promises broken and the dreams deferred—all because we're "in love" and would rather be slightly unhappy than completely alone.

So, what's love got to do with it? Everything! Especially in the manner we often dream of having it. Whenever you look for completion through another, you lay the foundation for a relationship that eventually will crumble because people undoubtedly will disappoint you. Even if they don't do it purposely or out of malice, they will do it just by virtue of being human. Two half-people simply make two half-people in a relationship. Only two whole people can have a whole relationship, and getting to that wholeness is a personal journey that we're all required to make on our own.

Being whole is hard work, and just like getting old, it's not something easily taken upon by sissies. It starts with knowing who you are. And even though that can take a lifetime, a lot of people never even begin the journey. There's a wonderful quote by writer Geneen Roth, which says: *Awareness is learning to keep yourself company.* We live in a world where keeping one's self company is not only difficult, but pretty much avoided. I know people who can't stand to be in the same room with themselves. My thing is this: If you can't stand being with you, what makes you think anyone else can?

There was a time when I believed in the romance of images—the image of the perfect woman, my "soul mate" so to speak—and I was very adamant about how I expected her to look, how tall she was, the color of her eyes and hair, and even her ethnicity. But the universe (always underrated for its sense of humor) kept delivering up an entirely different package. It took me a while, but I finally got it, and came to understand that you can be in love with anyone you open yourself up to. It doesn't matter whether they're young or old, short or tall, wealthy or without means, a different color, race, religion.

You find yourself seated next to him at a luncheon; stumble across her in a crowded room. Lock eyes in all the silly ways described in popular songs and old Harlequin romance novels. You're taken by surprise, because they're everything you imagine and wanted but different in a major way. Sometimes we miss them because we're still looking for the fantasy in our head, and don't see the real person standing right there in front of us.

Guys can be the worst offenders when it comes to this sort of thing because we're such visual creatures. The plain Jane girl with the nice shape and righteous disposition hangs out with us and becomes our best friend. But our heart aches for the "*Blonde in the Bleachers*" who whines constantly and is so high-maintenance that you have to take a second job. Keeping company with her is one major effort, but what the hell—she puts out regularly and is really nice to look at. Of course, vanity seeks its own level, and in this, both men and women get what they deserve. When you lie down with dogs, you get up with fleas and a whole bunch of ticks that you just gonna have to put up with.

Like I said, for a lot of us, falling in love is easy. Actor Pierce Brosnan, in a brief interview for *Preview* magazine, once lamented: "I love the romance of a good woman and the great rush of falling in love." I get that, but I have to say, I don't fall in love anymore. I'm still a romantic, and enjoy the rush, but I find that "growing into love" is a little bit more substantial. There's that same moment of attraction, but it's followed by a lot of paying attention and some healthy doses of skepticism. If I can make it past the initial body and face appraisal, I start to take notice of qualities that make her personable and unique. Something about the person stirs me.

I begin to appreciate and understand that when you first meet someone, you only experience the shell of who they are. You might notice the cut of their hair, the color of their eyes, and the line of their mouth. Later, as you get to know them better, the shell fleshes out; and the personality manifests itself in the way she brushes her hair back, the way her eyes sparkle when she smiles, or how reluctantly she intercepts a compliment. You notice the way she carries herself, and not so much what she wears, but how well she wears it. It's our awakening to the individuality of the person. The "spirit has become flesh," and we are charmed by its uniqueness.

When I find myself "growing in love," the other person becomes a muse and I become a more inspired lover. There are deeper parts of ourselves that we can share only with a lover. We share them from a place of safety, of knowing that they see us with eyes wide-open and an understanding of our imperfections and failings. We're too fragile to share these parts with just anyone. Insensitivity can break us. Thoughtlessness can bleed us like a knife. Indifference can dull our sharpness and take the edge off our creative best. I don't know if we truly understand the fear that comes with being human and putting ourselves out there. It's a wonderful feeling when two people can allow themselves to grow in spite of their differences.

It's so funny. We meet people, and we like the way they are, but for some reason we want to tweak them…just a little bit, as if we could make them better. We forget that who and how we are wasn't always that way. There was a time when we didn't like who we were or had become, and so we decided to change up. We tweaked ourselves to become the person we are today. We forget that process was a discarding of what others wanted us to be or expected.

It took me a long time to come to the understanding that most people love us for what we do for them or how we make them feel. And this is so easily confused with real love. However, loving us for who we are, regardless of how we make them feel or what we do, is so much harder. Who we are may not conform to who they want us to be, and giving up that ownership is what truly loving someone is all about.

## Memories of a First Love # 1

When I was twenty-one I fell in love. She was one of the most vivacious, intelligent and most daring women I have ever yet to know. Several years my junior, she became my first.

We were misty morning lovers. Rising early with the summer sun...sneaking out late...slipping into darkness. I watched her grow before my eye. Rescuing stray dogs abandoned along country roads; hiking down forgotten trails and railways, and crossing creeks overflowing with the sudden rush of April rain...in used bookstores searching out Poe, McKuen and Kavanaugh. With her, things were always real, seldom ordinary. Music was our second language and laughter became our first.

She taught me how to love—literally; how to kiss...deeply...softly...then stole my virginity in the back seat of my brother's car. A big part of the person I am today is because of her. The man, the lover, the poet...all found shelter in the warm crucible of her arms—burned alive with fire from the sensual press of her lips—smoldered into maturity in the cool, vacuous longing of her absence.

She taught me that passion wasn't always about forever...that it was sometimes more about the moment and the way we live our lives. Having known her has made all the difference. Women are indeed the true architect of men. This much I know is true

*But let us talk of passion that comes to us but once (maybe twice, if we are aware and attuned to its stirrings) and only to the brave. It comes with surrender and a willingness to abandon all the stuff that gets in the way of possibilities.*

*Passion is the thief of opportunity. That brief space where all rational thought is forsaken and we take hold of the moment...that instant we know to be filled with regret... but only if we fail to act.*

*Passion is never safe. Neither is it for the faint of heart. It is a wild flower flourishing in the landscape of untamed desires.*

(Excerpt from a Love letter 2000)

## All About Love...(continued)

Women have always devastated me. When you consider the fact that I consider myself to be a hopeless romantic—*hopeless* being the operative word here. You know that guy in all those movies who ends up saying and doing all those weird and outrageous things trying to win the girl he wants? Well, that would so much be me back in the day...well, possibly just the other day as far as that matters. I've made a fool of myself in the name of love so often that I'm not even embarrassed by it anymore. It's just that I'm really passionate when it comes to romance and love, which can be quite a contradiction, especially since I really do consider myself to be the head cheerleader for male "quirky-aloneness."

Still, when a woman really strikes my fancy, I have a tendency to pull out all the stops…and being a writer on top of it, well, that's inescapably a recipe for romantic insanity and some of the most creative, sensual and (often after-the-fact) embarrassing love letters ever to be written.

So, in the spirit of St. Valentine's Day, and for all those free-fall-lovers out there willing to sacrifice their integrity for that one (regardless of how shining the prose) that still got away, I offer up some of my best written love letters of years gone by. Of course, the names have been changed to protect me from the innocent.

## Love letter # 1

So, back in the early '90s, I met this girl, and we went to this really pedestrian Kevin Costner movie titled *For Love of the Game* (which, if I recall, was probably the beginning of Costner's steady descent into grade B moviedom). Anyway, there was a scene in the movie that had one of those lines, you know, the kind that makes women pause. And I remember the line so well, because in the moment he said it, even in the darkness, I could actually hear my date crack a smile.

So, this was probably our third date, and we hadn't even kissed yet, and I remember dropping her off and going home and thinking about that line, and her smiling. So the next morning I sat down and wrote her this letter:

*Dear Jeanette,*

*It's raining.*

*I can hear the raindrops tapping at my window like small stones tossed by some secret lover calling me out into the morning light. The sounds of early morning traffic are scarcely audible above the gentle hum of my computer, and my cat is softly creeping up the stairs stalking out the comfort of my touch.*

*Monday morning. I think about you. Startled out of dreams by the sudden shrieking of your alarm; surrendering the warmth of comfortable quilts for the cold, harsh brush of carpeted floors. I imagine you in flannel pajamas, or maybe silk lace bra and panties...or if I dare let my imagination run with the risqué...I can glimpse you briefly, naked and soft and warm.*

*I wonder. What are you thinking about as you shower, as the steam rises up around you. Are you thinking about the day ahead, the work undone? All the people who'll gather later around the office water cooler to talk about their children, debt and vacations, and how badly they all wanted to stay home today...just to listen to the rain.*

*I feel blessed...on this wet and wonderful Monday morning with autumn crying outside my window because summer has suddenly fled. I am sitting here...awash in the blue sea of my computer's glow...sheltered from the storm... thinking about you and wondering what you might look like in the morning.*

*For me...life is now. And now is always best to say the things we want and do the things we like. Unlike love, life makes no promises beyond the present moment...and here; in this moment...alone on this planet circling the sun...I am thinking about you and wondering...what you might feel like in the morning?*

*I am a poet. And few people understand what it means to be a poet in the world today.*

*To be a poet is to embrace that which is unreal. Because in today's reality based, technologically enhanced society, that which is unreal is unsure, and that which is unsure is full of mystery. And when life is full of mystery it tends to no longer feel safe and secure.*

*I am a poet.*

*I celebrate the mysteries of life; court its meanings and indulge its pleasures. I am amazed at the magnitude of its beauty... whether it's a sky ablaze with the blush of a setting sun...or a child suckling sleep in the hearth of its mother's arms...or the sweet, soft scent of woman sitting next to me...in a movie theater... in a darkness broken only by the whispering movement of a smile.*

*I am a poet Sometimes unsure...always unhurried...often at odds with a world that no longer suffers poets gladly I am not afraid to cry...to feel deeply... to laugh loudly...to love completely...foolishly...and with sheer abandon.*

*I am a poet. Here at this moment...in that darkness...on this morning... thinking about you and wondering, "How do you like to be kissed?"*

Later that week, after returning from an evening out, she handed me her keys to open the front door, and as she stepped inside she suddenly turned and threw her arms up around my neck and kissed me.

Ah, the power of good prose.

Postscript: Oh and how did she like to be kissed? "Slowly at first...then again with a special madness."

*All around me today, I see people dying from a lack of love and understanding. Drowning in a sea of unfulfilled promises, they cling tenaciously to the boat of past hurts and savage misunderstandings; waiting to be rescued, only to end up ship-wrecked once again....because in love, as in life, there are no guarantees.*

(Excerpt from a Love letter 2000

## A Few More Words...

It's funny. Even though we can't keep up with them, we still want 'em: younger women (eighteen to twenty-eight). They make our blood boil with their firm, taut bodies tucked into tight-fitting jeans. They invade our daytime dreams with their girlish ways and fire up our imagination with the guiltless spontaneity of their emerging sexuality. They make us horny.

I once worked with this young girl thirty years my junior. We teased and flirted with each other, and even though there was no way in heaven it could've worked for even a nanosecond, she simply gave out all the mixed signals needed in encouraging me to hit on her. (Of course, we guys are a unique species, capable of turning even our largest imperfection into that ego-tripping mantra: "She wants me").

Younger women—they make us older guys feel like boys again, but the truth is: We really need the mature understanding of older women, especially after forty. But every once in a while, the one that "should" have got away comes along and we become a child again, all clumsy and full of fire and the desire to impress her with cartwheels and hanging from trees.

## Love Letter #2

*Dear Annabel,*

*How you do so turn me on.*

*I am enchanted by the dichotomy of who you are: confident yet shy; beautiful yet plain. You are your most handsome without makeup...where each freckle amasses to give color to the portraiture of your face.*

*I have to confess...the other night when we talked, I suddenly realized that I had a hard time looking into your eyes. I felt distracted by their pale blue softness (the color of winter skies). They pulled me in. Teased me with their playfulness....haunted me with their weariness; stirred me with the secrets of their sensual mystery reflected in the aquamarine shimmer of their light.*

*I felt awkward....revealed, fearful that they peeped beyond the deep brown darkness of my own to winnow the desire rushing in my chest. Could you not detect the quickening of my breath? The pounding of my heart......my tale tell heart?*

*What a sight you were...all sleek in black...caught up in the mating ritual of pulling your hair back...exposing the pale curvature of your neck; the bow of your back unveiling the supple firmness of flesh just beneath the rise of your blouse.*

*You kept pulling your hair back...but each time a single lock escaped cascading down the length of your cheek to gently rest against the line of your smile.*

*What a sight I must have been....envious of that lone lock....that it should know the touch of your skin...the brush of your lips. Ten thousand angels swirled between us...just to keep me from falling to my knees before you... between the altar of your thighs...rising up to brush that lock aside...then taking hold to pull you near...closer....My God! The things I feel compelled to write. I become so reticent around you, which is not my usual way; a coward whose only response is in this gentle rush of words erupting in volcanic bursts across the blank screen of a white page.*

*You're right. Few men indeed dare write with such unbridled passion, and even fewer women still...will ever know the personal stroke of a poet's pen.*

*Yet, here we are. You....a young woman in need of romance...and I...an older man capable of rendering such.....what are romantics to do?*

Postscript: Needless to say…she broke my heart.

# Memory of a first love # 2

They say love is never as good as the first time. I guess it's true. Maybe because we're never as innocent as the first time: the first fumbled kiss, the rousing touch and pungent taste of another's mouth all alive and wet and sweet with the promise of forever.

The first body's ache…burgeoning…arms entangled...hands carousing...fingers slipping deep between the folds of silk and mystery. Breath pumping out hot and fevered; staccato whispers echoing like boom-box beats behind the ear; holding back…anticipation…straining to make it good even though there was nothing to compare it with.

Lying quiet afterwards, feeling spent; hearts pounding like low notes on piano strings, wondering what the other was thinking. Still warm and flush with the dog heat of passion. No. It's never as good as the first time.

Camille was my first.

At twenty-one, I was the last of my partners to lose his virginity. Of course, no one really knew. Like everyone else, I lied, pretended that it happened back when I was thirteen. Believe me, it wasn't easy. A lot of the guys in my neighborhood were experienced "cock hounds" and could sniff out even the most skilled pretender. But

I read a lot. Most of my stories plucked straight from the letter section of *Hustler* magazine. By the time I got through tellin' a story, those brothers be standin' around fidgeting; shoulders hunched, hands shoved deep into their front pockets; eyes flirting up and down the street looking for the first willing young lady to come along.

I knew back then I was going to be a writer. My storytelling was legendary in a neighborhood where having a say with words was as valuable as a carton of squares or a six-pack of Colt 45 malt liquor. I never lost at playin' the dozens.

It was the late '70s and early '80s; we used to hang out on the corner of Walnut and Spruce—the public square in my block of the world. That's where everything went on. That's where I met Camille…my first.

I know it sounds cliché, but it seems like just the other day. Good memories are like that, you know. Abandoned like sunken treasure and waiting just below the surface for a smell or taste or some old familiar jukebox song to rattle 'em loose and send 'em bobbing topside. Everything comes rushing back with the same intensity of the moment it first happened, and we find ourselves reliving it all over again.

With Camille, it was always the scent of lavender, faint and fresh and scarcely noticeable...the way honeysuckle hugs the air on sultry summer mornings heavy with the sweat of the day before. Lavender and sweet sixteen…that's how it was remembering Camille and the first time we made love.

*We lead such stale and passionless lives. Caught between childhood dreams and the realities of adulthood, we surrender ourselves to the mundane circumstance of living; held prisoner by the truths we think we know…seldom understanding that truth, like beauty, is often in the eyes of the beholder.*

(Excerpt from a Love letter 2000)

# One Last Word...Really...

And so, I continue to hold out for love. It's not a perfect love that I seek, nor an all-consuming love—but rather, a knowing and familiar love. I have known it in the embrace of my mother when I was a child, and in the shoulder hug of my father for a job well done. I have known it in the uncle who bandaged my bleeding knee and the sister who attended my first broken heart. I have known it in the gentle/roughhoused play of my brothers, and later in the friends who helped me move on the last day of the month when it rained so hard we couldn't see the new address.

It's a familiar love…felt in the handshake of the husband who trusted me to be alone with his wife and kids. It's an innocent love…found in the eyes of my first true love. It's a spiritual love… a worldly love…a human love.

How will I know if it's real? I will know.

# Love Letter # 3

*Beautiful Dreamer…*

*Where have you been, my Lady?*

*I have searched for you down cobblestone streets…through the dark alley ways of despair where dreams lay overturned and thrown about like so much garbage—in the vacant gaze of passersby; and in the reflective glare of storefront windows. I glimpse you once all bright and colorful and full of light—you smiled at me...but it was just a dream.*

*Since that day, I've searched you out on Westport Road. Eyes covered, nose press against the rain stained windows of back-street cafes—in checkout lines—down country roads—on the freeway in cars zipping by.*

*I thought I knew you....but all I really know is the way you smile, and the way you make my heart race every time I watch you climb the stairs and disappear.*

*Who are you really?*

*I thought I knew— but all I really know is the way your laughter hangs like scented flowers in rooms where you have been and me always one step behind.*

*If I could I would know you beyond the laughter of your smile; in that secret place kept inside the heart that only you would know.*

*There—inside that heartland—is all my want to wander, and unravel the mystery of who you really are.*

*To gaze into your dark-eyed skies and dance beneath the moon of your aspirations—to see you freckled and fresh in morning light; caught up in arms' embrace and the silent surrender of words spoken in a moment's passion.*

*If I could I would touch you in all the hidden places not known to any man, and kiss you in all the special ways unknown to any woman.*

*If I could...I would know you in all the ways of love.*

*For I am older...though young in body and spirit blessed...word/wise…a believer in dreams to come. Open of heart and mind…stolen long ago from a land across the sea, the warrior blood of the Motherland pulses proudly through my veins. I am nothing but a man...a boy...a child…a poet in a world that no longer suffers poets gladly.*

*Beautiful Dreamer...who are you really?*

*I will know you by your smile...by the way you say "Hello."*

# Of Men and Women
## I. Men

For far too long men have defined themselves in ways that have everything to do with how they are socialized and little to do with who they really are or want to be. It is only through conscious intention—a desire to do and be more than the role we have been prescribed—that we finally come to terms with the lies of a lifetime, and begin to live according to the truth and understanding of our own personal narrative.

The personal is also the most universal—in that it embraces the full spectrum of who we are as persons of a particular gender and all the habits inherent to group expression. How we express ourselves is in direct correlation to that dichotomy—the sum of who we are will always be twofold—as man/child, masculine/feminine. Accessing our two-faced nature is a balancing act predicated on just how much we love and understand ourselves. The more congruent we feel emotionally, the easier it is to except and respect the innumerable facets of our masculinity. Redefining ourselves to fit a truer representation of our gender makes it possible not only to recognize and value the uniqueness of who we are, but also to fulfill our role as partner/provider as it concerns our relationship to women.

Whether we choose to believe or not that women are the weaker sex, one thing is woefully apparent: Their condition and treatment in one of the most industrialized and progressive nations on the planet are a shameful indictment of our masculinity. Can we really concede to any plausible reason for a man to ever abuse his wife, girlfriend or daughter; whether mentally, emotionally or psychically?

God wasn't stupid in the architecture of the human species. We have a basic responsibility as the more physically stronger, to protect our most fragile—whether defined by circumstance of gender, ethnicity, orientation or class. And fragile should not necessarily be interpreted as meaning weak, but rather that which is delicate and easily broken. Human beings are such vessels.

It's been said that the opposite of love is not hate, but indifference (something we as men can be awful good at—if not purposely, then simply by way of habit). But, indifference as a means of engaging the world has many disadvantages, especially when it comes to the suffering of others. It's imperative that we re-reference the way we treat and address women. Skanks, hoes and bitches are not words we say to people we claim to love.

# 2. Women

I think the first and foremost casualty of the "gender war" came from focusing on our physical differences; we somehow misread those distinctions as deficits and proof of the other's inferiority. Of course, men have been doing this all along, and for feminist thinking to reflect this misguided perception was simply a huge mistake.

Is it really politically incorrect for me to say, that part of loving a man—for a

Woman—comes from the fact that he's stronger and can protect her? And that part of loving a woman—for a man—is knowing that she's the physically weaker of the two and needs that protection. This I believe is hardwired into us because of our physical differences, and is so linked to a man's need of being a hero. Maybe I'm stupid (and I have been known to read more into some things than there actually were), but there's not a man alive who hasn't at one time gathered his lady up in the muscular valley of his arms and felt the twinge of satisfaction that he was providing her some kind of respite.

On the flip side, there's not a woman on the planet who at one time or another hasn't felt the sinuous comfort of that sanctuary and nestled herself even deeper into its fleshy folds....and not for one second did either of them ever feel that something about the other was diminished.

As with most things in life, "protection" shouldn't be so narrowly defined. Being understanding and supportive can also be forms of protection. If a man is mindful and encouraging of the woman in his life, he protects her by validating her sense of self-worth; allowing her to grow beyond the stereotypical limitation imposed by the larger society. Really strong and confident men are never threatened by another's capabilities, whether they're male or female. And honestly, what man doesn't want a strong capable woman as a wife, mother or partner? We know there's nothing more endearing (especially when we have the sniffles), than being taken care of by a woman who loves us when we're having a serious "sissy moment"—and we do have plenty of them.

But there's also a larger benefit. It's when a woman is supported that she feels the most loved and valued, and from that position of edification she becomes more than just a mother or wife—she becomes a consecrated human being. By embracing her power and acknowledging her distinct nature, she accepts the liability of what we all know (but seldom won't admit), that women are the architects of men and own a unique position in the raising of their boy children. Fathers do have their place, but the assignment of mother is an intrinsic one given out by nature. If we want better and more enlightened men, then it's incumbent upon them to be better and more enlightened women—not only in the way they mother their daughters and sons, but more so in the manner they challenge their husbands and lovers. And they can do this by holding themselves, as well as the men in their life, to a higher standard. When a woman speaks from that place which is the true source of her power, she brings into existence a force capable of transforming the very nature of our humanity.

Understand, ladies, that men will get away with only that which you will allow them to. You need to realize that the source of your power lies not between the cleft of your legs, but between your ears and within your hearts, and it's your responsibility to speak from that source with a might that will rock and reshape the world. If you aren't honest in your self-assertions, if you fail to bring the inimitability of your gender—of what you are into the mix—then I'm afraid to tell you: Nothing will ever change. You will simply continue to be paid lip service, and the very essence of who you are, will continue to be brokered in a marketplace that will forever undervalue you as an essential human being.

## 3. Embracing Our Better Selves

I believe few women today are in need of being saved. That doesn't mean they don't need men to be heroes in their lives. They just need them to be heroic in other ways: as loving fathers and available husbands and partners; as men willing to share the burden and embrace the responsibility that comes naturally with a commitment to engage life.

I think part of the answer to this dilemma is for both sides to give up on the PC bullshit that has commonly come to be defined as fairness. What was initially created to accommodate the inequities of the past has somehow twisted itself into an instrument for censorship and a denial of some of our most obvious distinctions. I truly believe if we can "man and woman up" in our efforts to reconcile ourselves regarding gender, then we also might be able to reconcile ourselves regarding race, orientation, class and just about anything else that tends to marginalize and divide us.

However, this only will come about if we, as men, are willing to open ourselves to other possibilities—to challenge our deeply embedded sense of narcissism—to embrace our better selves by inviting women into the mix and onto a playing field that's level and fair and fully considerate of our differences.

This is not a contradiction. It's quite possible to be both equal and different. It simply evolves from an understanding that who and what we are is in no way any less than the other; that we each bring our individual pluses and minuses to the equation in an effort to decipher the best answer.

When we accept the responsibility of being the physically stronger, and choose to carry the mantle of Hero, then it's truly incumbent upon us to step up and do so. What this means is that we can't even begin to entertain thoughts of irresponsibility when it comes to the keeping of women and children—and I mean that in the most literal sense of expression.

I've heard it said that the definition of greatness is when everything that came before you becomes obsolete—and everything that comes after has your mark.

We have marked the world before. As men, we have left our footprints on the surface of the moon, and upon the backside of those who were weaker than us. For every great achievement there has also been a failing—a failing to live up to that greatness—but we're a different breed now. We know more about the human condition and who we are than at any other moment in history. So the time has come to redefine ourselves...as husbands...as fathers...as men.

The future will bear our mark. We will be heroes again. To that end, when all is said and done, we will be able to honestly confess to the women in our lives: I'm the kind of man that your mother always wanted you to meet. But even more than that, I'm the kind of man that my mother always wanted me to be.

# PART THREE
## Poetry as Confession

"There are three things men can do with women: love them, suffer for them,
or turn them into literature. I've had my share of success
and failure at all three."
-Stephen Stills

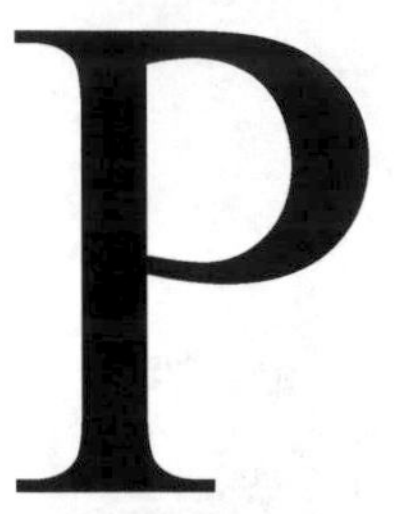oetry is confession.

But instead of a priest, you sequester yourself before the blank page of an empty screen; asking repentance for crimes committed against the heart. You kneel before the altar of experience, seeking absolution for the mishandling of dreams—yours and others—because there are things that only simile and metaphor can forgive.

I think I'll always consider myself to be a poet first. It was poetry that midwifed my creativity and delivered rhyme into my life. Fiction and nonfiction were twin siblings that showed up later, and I parent them with a similar passion. However, when it comes to poetry, well, it's like that old Smothers Brother's line: "Mom always liked you best."

In poetry we come clean of our regrets—and there will always be regrets: regrets for not keeping promises, regrets for inventing lies, regrets for not kissing the girl when she clearly offered us the opportunity. We learn from these mishaps; in the meaning we gather from people, places and things.

In the end it absolves us of nothing and everything.

## For the Women

### Poems

**D**o you know how long I have been waiting for you? And do you know how long you have been searching for me? So there I was, standing at the peripheral of your life...waiting for you to notice me...waiting for you to say...yes!

## Excuse Me

This morning as you stood
swaddled in sunlight
the nature of your personality
once more revealed
in the stories you told…
with knowing ease..
your voice
a soft song against
the white walled silence
of those
who are no strangers to your words…
I listened
and felt the love you carry there
stage right of the dreams
you hold in places
of the heart:
the mother love
the sister love…the young
girl love
all grown up into a woman;
the mama love
all proud and warm and kind
the same love you give to me
upon arrival
waiting at the door
waiting for that
soft embrace
that says
I care.
So, excuse me
as I fall
for
you

**What She Needs**
For Shannon

She wants the moon and the stars
but what she needs are
soft kisses and kind words to
show that she is equal in celestial movement and the way she shines.
She wants to be free of money and time
but what she needs
are hands to hold and
dark eyes that sparkle and see her
naked in morning light; capturing forever the way she smiles...
She wants sunshine days and crystal nights
but what she needs are
summer solstice and winter equinox
to know that she is seasonal
in the way she feels
      and
she needs
cool side glances,
a muscular/soft
      warm
body to hold and
press into…
the touch and feel
of love's sweet sweat;
the heat
of love's first fire..

She wants world peace
but what she needs
is just to know
that she is loved.

## I Grew into Loving You

For Chris

I grew into loving you…
sad child at the door of my heart…
your eyes
drained
of their pure color
a faded blue
against the jaundice sky…
having loved and lost
the memory still fresh,
the hole
an open wound.
Yet…I grew
into loving you,
"girl/child unsafe
in a world of men"…locked
in isolation…
dreams held hostage
to a past of pain and hurt;
eyes wide shut yet open
to the meter of my heart…
the halted speech
staccato murmurs and
words to raw
to be spoken.
Still…
I grew into loving you…
hand on heart
a better woman
I've yet to know…
your reticent smile
your furrowed brow
the kiss of your voice
a soft whisper
in the dark.
We were meant
to be lovers.

**Sky Dolphin**
For Gretchen

Sky Dolphin
dreams
of blue water skies
and Starfish brite-nights
cloud sailing along hot pink horizons...
She
dances
skip stoning on ocean waves
cold water fresh
on beaches littered with yester-
daydreams
and shells that sparkle
with iridescent
highlights
like
the colors in her hair...
She
blushes
breaking waves
with storm cloud whiteness
where gulls dip and dive
and pierce the heart of heaven
with their tears...
She
walks on air
heavy with heartfelt laughter
ship wrecked and stranded
she sees tomorrow waiting
like maritime ghosts
and knows that
p e a c e
is but the dream of those
who've looked
into the face of God
and
still believe

**Poem**
For Julie

**One**

I like the rush
of liking you…
having known you from afar
I didn't know the true
color
of your eyes
nor the way your nose
wrinkled
when you smiled;
I didn't know
your laugh was like a giggle
or that the voice of your eyes
spoke in whispers
that only I
could hear.

**Two**

I like the rush of liking you…
the innocence girl
in a grown up body
who still believes in dreams
and
the kindness of strangers;
eyes wide open
arms extended
still willing to embrace an unsure world.
I didn't know
the true depths of your heart
nor the ease at which you come to tears;
I didn't know
how alone you felt
with people swirling 'round.

## Three

I like the
rush of liking you…
the soft sound of your voice
in the dark of night
the kiss of your words before sleep.
I didn't know
the true value
of a woman's spirit
having known you from afar
coming into focus I see
a whole other person
too real
to be ignored.
I like the rush
of liking you…knowing you...
touching you…
I like the rush
of loving you…
I didn't know
any one woman
could ever make
me feel this way.

**I Remember When**

For Alicia

**I** remember when
I use to make love to
the pounding of the rain and
the beating of your heart…and how
we g a s p e d for breath
beneath passion's downpour and
in/between
the lightning flashes of a hot and humid sky. **A**nd
I remember
how we drenched ourselves in ecstasy…
arms entwined…bodies entangled…
and the taste of sweat was as sweet as spring water
as salty as the sea; and
your breathing was like thunder
and your sighing like the wind
and
your body arched with lightening quickness
a c r o s s the landscape of my thighs…and the storm
that was you…grew closer..
wilder..wet…striking once
twice
where upon the third time
your voice lit the darkness
and the thunder roared…and the earth moved..
and our bodies quaked and quivered
in a swirl of clouds &
emotions…**t**hen
just as quickly…the clouds receded;
the passion passed…and the storm that was you
subsided into pleasant sounds and rumblings.
**A**nd
I remember wet kisses…deep……and how
loving you was like a sudden storm
that came and went; where afterwards
we would splash in warm puddles
of easy conversation…
washed clean
and left
renewed.

**Blue Jeans Poem**

For Kris

I found
your old blue jeans
the other day
the ones you wore that time
when we were last together...remember?
Torn at the knee
and frayed at the ankles..still
wrapped and neatly folded
by the sales lady who complimented me
then went on to tell you
how well the new pair fit.. and how
she envied your girlish curves
and
wispy smile..then
rated you a 10 at 33…which
she really didn't have to say
because the sale
had already been made
by the way you looked
as(s) you walked away
with me not far
behind.

I found
your old blue jeans
the other day
still folded and wrapped and tucked up under
the front seat at the back of the car...
and all this time I've been missing you
not seeing you
sitting across from me
yet somehow feeling your presence
like a reflection in the side view mirror
where objects appear
c l o s e r
than they really are.
I found your old blue jeans...just yesterday
and in/between the folds and creases
the scent of you was fresh and clean
and sweet
as our first kiss...
I wrapped the legs about my neck
to try and pull you close to me
and taste
the soft clear memory
of when we
last made love.

**Afrika In Your Smile**
For Wanjiku

I see Afrika
when you smile...
in the sway of your hips
there is rhythm
that birthed
the Watusi...the Shing a ling..
and the Hustle....on dance floors
all across these Americas…and
I see Afrika
when you smile...
in the song of your voice
there is melody
that speaks to me
of Makeba..and Whitney
..and Chaka Kahn...
in sun lit rooms
full of joy & singing
and the belly laugh
of a happy people…and
I see Afrika
when you smile...
in the coarse silk of your hair
in the full pout of your lips
in the soft brown
light of your eyes
I see the tears of my people
And know too that
you are my Sister...
'cause... I see Afrika
when you smile.

**Brown Skin Girl**
For Josephine

Brown skin girl
with your red licorice smile and
chocolate color dreams....
I have known your sweetness
in the way Mama braids hair and
softly calls me
by my whole full name...
in the way Papa sings the blues and
little baby brother jumps hoops and
big sister Bertha shouts in the choir on
a summer's Sunday afternoon.
Brown skin girl
with your red licorice smile and
chocolate color dreams....
I have known your sweetness
in the way Grandma patches quilts and
bakes me sweet potato pies...
in the way Grandpa walks his walk
and says his howdy-dos
in the ways Aunt Josie and
Aunt Mae Mecall me "sweet child" and "baby boy, all
grown up gonna break a lot of hearts someday"
Brown skin girl
with your red licorice smile
and you deep dark chocolate dreams and
your tight corn-rowed hair and
your bright pearly whites and your heart
stuffed full with the promise of a
hand-me-down love...
Brown skin girl...gonna make me wanna love..
gonna make me wanna sing...
gonna make me wanna shout...
"Hallelujah."

**You Shot Me Down One Day**
For Rebecca

You shot me down one day
and like a wounded bird I fell
to the
mis/conceptions of your words.
A
cosmopolitan hunter
you came…taking aim
upon the wild creature of my masculinity…
your
arrogance well oiled…polished
& hidden...
camouflaged
behind the colorful
carousel of your smile…
your predator smile.
I
felt the blast
even as your tongue tripped the trigger
and
your lips
e x p l o d e d
in an onslaught of leaden words
clipping my passing in mid-flight…
&

even as I fell…crashing down
earthbound;
wings rent and broken
from your sudden assault…

I realized then
That no
one/person
would ever treat me so again.
You
shot me down one day
the vagueness of your sanity
b l a z i n g
in the noon-day sun..
and since then;
I've often wondered
If you ever understood…
that
being a man
is just as difficult
as
being a woman…that the
casual show of ego
conceals an inner doubt…and that
even as you've cried..
I've cried too…
perhaps for the same reason.
Yes
you shot me down
one day…
….but I survived.

**<u>A Woman's Geography</u>**
For Natalie

There's something about
a woman's back
the line of spine
a lattice track
nestled between arched shoulders…
stair-stepped
from neck to bottom
where dimples and curves meet
in soft designs
both round
and rousing.
There's something about
a woman's back
whether smooth or blemished
or brown-skin-finished…
the curvy hips
the span of legs
a supple stretch
from length
to width.
I have trekked the landscape
of your body with my eyes..
retraced
the footprints
left by other lovers…

… from
breast to groin...pressed
against the silk of your thighs
        …the curve of your back
        a fetal question mark
        against my line
        of chest…
        between the fold of
        sweat/stained sheets
                        the memory
                        of a love
        I've never known.
There's something about
a woman's back
        whether pale and freckled
        or
soft/skin speckled…
a tattooed star rising
above one shoulder…the dark of your hair
                          falling
in gentle cascades…against the soft
of your skin…
                the blush of your eyes…
   the quick of your breath how
   I long to kiss…you
                            right there.

**Girl/Child**
For Gretch

I knew you when
you were knee-high
to the beating of my heart
girl/child
in an unsure world..
you came to me
through a mama's love
with an innocence so rare
I've not known since…
you…girl/child
with your secrets ways
inhabiting the space between dreams
and
other peoples
reality…
your smile
an easily given gift
right before you
laugh
that
laugh
that
sealed the deal
on my love forever.
I lost you mid-
-sentence from
the narrative of my life…
High/jacked by
circumstance…we drifted off
you stumbling thru Babylon…
me…directionless
with no true north…always wondering
what became of you…
girl/child.

I found you
18 yrs.+ 1
hiding in plain site
the familiar arc of
your smile
a fond remembrance…the
color of your eyes
much like my own..
strong-willed and soft-hearted…
fair-minded and joy/full
we share a childhood past
of bedtime tales and summer colds
tight hugs and cheek kisses
stories written
in broad strokes
on Big Chief tablet paper…
that you
would know me still
as father
to another man's daughter
is a warm delight and
testimony to who you are
that same person
I recall
when
you were but a girl/child
knee-high to the beating
of my
heart.

**Dabbling in Chocolate**
For Kim

She likes her vanilla bread
dabbling in chocolate
her Eurocentric sense/abilities
easily offended
by the visceral reality of
those who's opposite
attracts
and
repels.

**I Want To**
For Julie

I want
to lay in your arms...
the way a cat
lays in sunshine
all comfortable and loose
s t r e t c h e d out
and y a w n i n g
legs tossed
casually across the lap
soaking up the heat
of your
morning smile.

**Sniper Eyes**
For Beth

She
wears
amber highlights in her hair
Summer hot
& cool as brothers
hangin’ out on 18th ‘n’ Vine
She
sweats
sweetness in the way she walks
taking parting shots
from
behind dark glasses
with
her sniper eyes...
I see her peering out
at me
from just beneath
the cross+hairs
of her lashes.

**For The Children**

When the people enter laughing
coming in from off the street
come to me my child my darling
I will make the bitter sweet
when the people
enter laughing
pretend there's only you and me.

When the children cease their playing
trading toys for games of war
run to me my child my darling
Where there's peace and nothing more
when the children
cease their playing
come and we shall close the door.

When the world is through with turning
Slowly spinning 'round to die
Turn to me my child my darling
If you feel the need inside
when the world
is through with turning
come and learn the reason why.

When all love seems gone forever
buried 'neath the shifting sands
hold me close my child my darling
give your best to understand
when all love seems gone forever
take the world
into your hands.

## Ode to Relationships

### One

While I was
grinding on girls
you were
bumping with boys…
unaware that life was
preparing us
for love
we grew up
looking down
and over our shoulders
for dreams
that were yet to be.

### Two

While I was stealing sweet kisses
you were
breaking brave hearts…
cultivating lovers
beneath
the spell of your full moon eyes;
knocking
others to their knees
with the wiles of
your
Cheshire smile.

### Three

We were partners in crime
time bandits
living parallel lives;
you the master thief
stealing kindness…
both
breaking
and
broken hearted.

## **Four**

I was
not as cool as you;
though older
by a degree of fives
and far from fly…
I manage to survive the loss
of love and other obsessions
and
knowing this now
I would have been no match for
the ruse of your
girlish
smile.

## **Five**

Still…While
you were
buoying for boys….
I was
goo goo for girls;
peeping in bedroom windows
snatching glances from a far
thru doors ajar
and
curtains purposely left open
in well lit rooms
by daughters who
pretended not to know
…showing
off their fine forms
inherited from mothers
whose vigilant husbands
patrolled the neighborhood
searching out
us way-
ward
boys.

**Six**

I was (am
still)
that voyeur/boy who
searched out love's mystery
in every crooked smile;
and discovered that poetry
not only saved souls
but easily pried
the heart and thighs
of young ingénues
looking for affection
in the reflections
of someone
else's
eyes.

**Seven**

A fair-weather
player…
haunted by
words;
crying out
to define myself
in ways that only I understood;
just another
lost brother
whose dreams died with
Malcolm and
Martin & the sister down the street
who stole my heart
then refused
to give it
back.

**Eight**

Life barred me
and scarred me early
in a game that claimed
my spirit for a price
I was unwilling to pay.
The color
of my skin
akin
to Cain;
only Abel
to find revenge
in the cool embrace
of my oppressor's
daughters…
prying their pale hearts
apart
from the clutches
of their stark
white
withering
ways.

**Nine**

They were willing
captives…all;
fair skinned
with devil blue eyes
and
butch cropped hair;
products of a revolutionary time
a state of mind
anchored in the emerging
rhetoric of
self and
other.

## Ten

One in particular
sought me out and
taught me about
the ways of love
and lust;
her brave heart
a testament
to a spirit
I've
not known since…
another
stole my heart
with a child on the side
making me father
to another man's daughter
then divorced me
Christmas eve
for
a younger man…
her worst/best gift
ever.

## Eleven

And still another
fooled me
with my own eyes
into believing
the lies I told myself
about who she was
or
wanted to be;
her words a stinging reminder
that
anger can out last
love and even
kill
it's
possibilities.

**Twelve**

So…
50 + years
and/a half
to the day;
you eventually
found your way
to the page
where my soul laid prone
and open…
the man revealed…
no
longer haunted by
words
held back
in
non-
belief.

**Thirteen**

You…
with your reticent smile
woman/child
your slim/finger
hands
stroking the looms
where language is stretch
into sentences;
then woven
into stanzas of
5's
and
sevens.

**Fourteen**

You…
challenged me
with your vocabulary
in a hand-me-down language
that was not my own
but pressed upon
the tongue
of those
who four scores
and several hundred
years ago
were brought
to these shores in chains
under the precept of a new
nation…
with
old
idea

**Fifteen**

Scribes
from
Opposing tribes…
we bridged the divide
with late nite talk
and tentative walks
in opposing direction…
testing one an/other
and challenging
our fears
and unknowing;
we waged
a kinder war—
surrendering
and
remembering
that in love
all indeed is
fair.

## Sixteen

Night and day
was
too obvious a metaphor
for the distinctions
we inhabited.
I was use
to walking on water
and you
were just beginning to tread
the ocean of misspent
desires and
unfathomable
possibilities.

## Sixteen

You
wondered
if I could
see you thru the smoke
of my dark/brown eyes.
I saw you
and more
in the words you spoke
and the way your laughter
danced
away the darkness;
in the manner
you clothed yourself,
and in the way
you prize
the heart of the little
girl with your
same slim/finger
hands.

**Seventeen**

I
See you
even now
in morning dreams
where only we are there
and
the way you say
my name
makes me
catch my breath
and stirs my groin
with memory
of a passion left
unspent.

**Eighteen**

You were (are
still)
everything
I never knew I wanted
in a lover/friend…
fierce and
challenging; easily
given to
tears.

**Nineteen**

I love
having you in my arm
nestled between the hinge
of my shoulder…
the soft of your cheek
against the plank
of my chest…the silk of your hair
a pillow
for my face.

**Twenty**

There
(was
is still)
a comfort
in
the nearness of you
that calms my restless spirit;
a respite
from the fears
that haunt me nights
when I'm alone.

**Twenty-one**

I love
having you in my
heart
like this…
the after/words we share
after making love
(was
is)
and will always be
some kind of wonderful
that I have seldom known
nor may
ever know
again.

# PART FOUR
## A Season of My Own

*"Live in each season as it passes: breath the air, drink the drink, taste the fruit."*
*-Henry David Thoreau*

# PROLOGUE:
## Engaging the Muse

Just about the time I stopped blogging, I lost my job. Once again, writing became my salvation, but this time in the form of journaling. I have to admit, my journaling had always been rather sporadic and a little bit schizophrenic, but only in the sense that it was more like "free writing," streaming all the BS out of my head as a precursor to getting down to the more serious stuff of crafting a manuscript.

As with blogging, I decided to take a different approach—making my journal writing a conscious exploration between myself and the world—as if talking to a trusted friend or colleague, and applying the tenets of my craft to every line of thought—to make it both conversational and artful in its presentation. This was going to be my opportunity to really get in touch with myself...on every conceivable level.

Losing my job of seven years was a fairly traumatic experience. At the time the economy was like a drowning man treading water and caught up in the undertow of staggering disbelief. Corporations were dumping people in Titanic proportions—no one was hiring.

So, like any sane, creative person with limited funds and resources...I decided to take the year off. Not that I could really afford to do so, but unlike many who at the time were swaddled in credit card debt and inflated home equity loans, the only debt I carried was a mortgage that could easily be afforded on a part-time job. It seems, all of my choices—from being childless and having never married, to the work I did in supporting myself as an artist and writer—were, regardless of their consequences, conscious choices made with complete mental and emotional disclosure. I had learned early on that true leadership began with leading myself.

That year off was a gift from the Universe. It would become a time of unflinching reflection—in gathering my thoughts and reassessing the content as well as the context of where I had come from and where I was now going. To do this, I incorporated two techniques used in psychology and counseling: "looking back" and "looking forward" as well as being present in my current life's situation. Journaling, like most writing, isn't a linear process. The days may pass single file in a forward direction, but the thoughts recorded are often poignant vignettes snatched from the past and stitched into the tapestry of our current life circumstance.

Journaling is self-discovery. There's no way around it. You can't put pen to paper without exposing yourself in real and significant ways. That's why the violation of such privacy feels like an act of acute betrayal. But this writing I did was meant to be shared—to connect with others in its familiarity with the things we go through simply by being alive.

In response to a question from PBS talk show host Tavis Smiley, Lupita Nyong'o, star of the award-winning movie, *12 Years A Slave*, aptly replied, "We are not as individual as we think we are." I agree. Whether fresh from the cave or the hands of creation, the human element is both unique and mundane in its experience. And there's so much that happens during the course of a year that we never take account of: holidays, and how we approach them; the birth and death dates of the people we know or knew; current states of affairs and events; the history of our times unfolding before our eyes.

Having come of age during one of the most turbulent times in the history of our nation, I sought to answer: where had been my place at that time…and what affect did those times have on me and those around me? What do I remember about my father, my mother, my four brothers and two sisters? How did their loving affect me? And what about all the other people who traversed the landscape of my life: the quirky teachers, the brief childhood associations from grade school through high school; the neighborhood I grew up in and the character who inhabited it?

We seldom acknowledge these things; accept in passing (and more often when lying on our deathbed)—rarely realizing their impact or any deeper meaning. By focusing my journaling, I became more self-aware—something that I really wanted to be at this third chapter. The end game of my life. My journaling became a unique and personal experience. Thoroughly cathartic and fully mindful of what I was seeking to accomplish, which was: a better understanding of myself and my place in the world.

I take refuge in writing. And journaling for me was memoir writing, not only as a way of rediscovering myself, but as a way of getting back to my original passion: my love root. Those calendar days would fondly become A Season of My Own.

*"In the depth of winter, I finally learned that within me there lay an invincible summer."--Albert Camus*

# DECEMBER

## S M T W T F S

Late last night a small storm blew in from the north, lightly dusting the trees and streets in a powdery confection of white. Every now and then wild winds flagged the branches just outside my bedroom window, making creepy scratching sounds all night long. I think it must have been the raking of the trees that eventually nudged me awake, although these days it really doesn't take much.

First snows have always signified to me that winter has arrived. Not by calendar days or phases of the moon, but rather nature on her own terms, though nowadays she seems to be having a much harder time at it. They say global warming will literally change the way the seasons ebb and flow by about ten miles or so every year, and should that truly be the case, then here in the Land of Oz we might not see our first snow till early January. I'm not quite sure if I like that. Still.

I used to feel a sense of urgency to living...as if I had little time to squander on people and events that no longer moved me forward toward greater aspirations—probably because I was such a late starter when it came to so many things. Sidetracked by the vulgarities of living for the moment, I was often distracted by the myriad choices that moment afforded me. Or maybe it was just the lessening of self that quickened the need to accomplish all that I could now...though these days, once again, that no longer seems to be the case. Regardless, sometimes I fear that the sins of the past have come back to visit me both psychically and mentally.

When I was young, about thirteen or so, an old acquaintance of my mother's came to visit. She was a bold, beautiful black woman with darkly made up eyes, flawless caramel-colored skin and a joyfulness that was evident in the quick display of her smile. In the neighborhood where I grew up, it was whispered that she was one of those rare people blessed with the gift of sight and prophecy.

I remember how she turned to me when I entered the room and my mother paused to introduce her. She looked at me with soft, faraway eyes and put her hand on my shoulder and murmured, "I see a star above his head." Then turning to my mother, she smiled and said, "This boy's gonna do something great someday." They both sort of laughed and then walked away, but I remember that day and the words she whispered so clearly. I am haunted by that memory…by the casual escape of her words.

Perhaps, this is not such a good thing to happen to a child whose fertile mind is given to dreams and schemes, and the wild imaginings of things that go bump in the night. Since that day I have looked for meaning in many things, hoping to catch a glimmer of some greater purpose disguised in the common experience of my day-to-day life. And to this day that purpose eludes me.

Anyway, I digress. These are simply melancholy musings…on a wintry melancholy morning. Late last night a small storm blew in from the north. First snows always make me feel this way.

*"What we remember from childhood we remember forever,*
*permanent ghosts, stamped, inked,*
*imprinted, eternally seen."*
*-Cynthia Ozick*

* * *

In keeping this journal, I have decided not to write about the mundane circumstance of my everyday life—that's too redundant—a pattern of getting up and going about the dictates of the day. Such a recording of events is as dull as "Tweeting," uninteresting and self-indulgent, and best left in the realm of keeping a diary.

Instead, I have come to realize that woven between the many strands that attach the hours to my days are tiny revelations and accidental insights that help me make sense of my place on the planet. All the "now" moments that make up our lives, but are rushed through so quickly that they seldom register as memory. This is what I want to record—paying attention, not so much to the details, but to the particulars of each unfolding event and chance encounter.

Awareness is the key to this type of journaling. Actually, awareness is key in soliciting the most out of every circumstance of our day-to-day lives. Like this morning, when I rolled out of bed and got dressed. I was aware of how fitful my sleep had been and how tired I still felt. But going ahead and doing my morning workout rejuvenated me in a way that is becoming acutely familiar.

I notice how much I like the look of sweat on my body and the feel of heat in my muscles. I like knowing that I have endurance and a sense of myself in that moment. I like breathing deep and expending myself to the point of exhaustion—then starting all over again. At nearly sixty-two, it's not about feeling young, but rather about feeling fit—and that pleases me.

There are blessings that I truly understand and appreciate at this place and time in my life.

* * *

This morning the air is heavy with humidity. The clouds are dark and gray and filled with the threat of impending rain…as if the sky were simply waiting… holding back tears. Or maybe it's just me, reflective in these early hours of shadow and light and rain.

I wonder: How does one live in a world of common men? How do brave hearts that feel deeply and surrender easily to the stirring of countless desires and unimaginable possibilities—survive in a world of fear and doubt; where chance encounters and purposeful meeting are held in check by our lack of faith that things could possibly be more or better?

It's been said, "For lack of a vision the people perish."

* * *

The discovery of self is constantly happening in small moments and experiences. I see that more clearly now than at any other time in my life, and this writing—this introspection here and now at this time and place—is my own personal moral imperative.

I get it now; change is the only constant in life (a troubling oxymoron but true none the less). And the more honest I am about my part in relations to the crimes committed against my life, the sooner I will be transformed and capable of reclaiming what mythologist Joseph Campbell was so fond of calling: "the life that is waiting for us."

*                    *                    *

One seldom gets the opportunity for introspection. We live such crowded lives of rushing and doing. I think what makes it harder for me is that I've never been fully engaged in that way of living. I've always moved at a much less metered pace than those of my peers. Following that star that was separate from other constellations, I listened to the music of my choice, ignored sports and consistently loved from afar.

I was more than just a late comer to a lot of things; most of the time I was simply DOA (disinterested on arrival). And I find that to be true even today. However, it's not that I lack the ambition for the technological comforts of our times; it's just that I find many of them distracting and unnecessary.

I prefer the old-school habits of handwriting checks and paying my bills by mail, browsing the video store in search of a good movie, and shopping during the wee hours of the morning—days ahead of the weekend rush—each of those things a conscious choice…my way of inhabiting the planet.

It's so easy to surrender control to the trends of our modern times…to give in to the marketing…to sell our souls to the devil in the retails. And it's such a subtle surrender that one scarcely can recall when it all first began.

Don't get me wrong. I have no real quarrel with modern technology. I'm a writer, and I really enjoy my laptop computer and the freedom it allows me to create and edit anywhere I choose. I'm just a big believer in retaining some semblance of control over how that technology segues into my life. There's nothing useful or cathartic about being overwhelmed.

I'm beginning to understand, more than ever, just how important it is to define myself by the way I live and the things I choose to do.

*                    *                    *

This morning the girl behind the checkout counter made an indescribable face as she lifted a bag of Brussels sprouts before weighing them. "What are these?" she asked curiously, searching for a price. I told her, and she continued with a response that rated the vegetable just below peas and spinach.

As I exited the store, I thought about our exchange and the things she said. Growing up, I was very particular about eating. I hated any kinds of beans, cornbread, collard greens or their likes (all cultural mainstays). And don't get me started on beets and turnips—I can complain for days.

But the palate of youth is defined by our physiology, something that I clearly understand now. Illuminating taste in her extraordinary treatise *A Natural History of the Senses,* writer Diane Ackerman explains that our "Taste buds wear out every week to ten days, and we replace them, although not as frequently over the age of forty-five." She goes on to affirm that our palates become "jaded" as we get older, "...blunted by years of gourmandizing or trying to eat hot soup before it cools." This sort of makes youth more impetuous than I ever imagined.

This morning's checkout conversation touched off several things that had me thinking out loud to myself on the way home. The first was being able to dislike something without even knowing what it was. It's true what they say about opinions: Everybody has one. But having one about something you don't know has got to be some kind of crazy.

We do this all the time, though, and most often with those who are different from us in ethnicity, race, and orientation—passing judgment purely upon appearances and clichéd assumptions. It's not that stereotypes lack truth; it's just that they're so incomplete in their assessment. Cultural behaviors notwithstanding, we are truly more alike than not.

To be honest, most things in life are an acquired taste—in regards to not only the foods we dislike, but even to how it relates to institutions and ideas, and most importantly to the diversity of people we encounter. I can't begin to list the number of times I started out not really caring for someone only to have them end up a fond acquaintance.

We snap to judgment too quickly and too often, short-circuiting myriad possibilities. I want to free myself of that habit.

* * *

I grew up the middle child in a family of seven: five boys and two girls. The youngest of my brothers was killed in an auto accident early on in his life; another struggled with issues of mental health. The next to the oldest of my brothers married just out of high school, fathered two children and then divorced several years later. The oldest of my brothers (the most soft-spoken and amicable of us all) was a lanky, six foot four inches and academically inclined; he graduated in the early '70s as the first Black lawyer in our county.

The oldest and youngest of all my siblings were, respectively, my two sisters; who never married and ended up taking care of my father after my mother passed away. We were all pretty close back then, but these days we're only as close as the distances that separate us.

I was also the middle child in that cluster of boys, and probably the truest reflection of both my mother and father (which is often said of middle children). Rebellious and fiercely independent, I started out being held in check by Sunday school and an unspoken yearning to be a preacher. Back in those early years I spent an awful lot of time alone, communing with God and nature, and drinking in scripture as if it were some sacred elixir.

But the Civil Rights Movement of the '60s and the counterculture movement of the '70s proved to be both my undoing and my salvation. Looking back, it was simply a natural but bizarre progression…from boyhood activist to semi-revolutionary, pot-smoking hippie non-conformist. I supported myself not so much by working hard as by working more shrewdly; dropping out of college for jobs that paid well and offered the greatest amount of freedom in pursuing my passion for writing, art and, later on, photography.

I was published early without pay. Worked for a time as a counselor with abused and neglected children; traversed the hilly highways of my home state as a Weight Officer, chasing renegade truckers and overweight eighteen-wheelers in a really cool, dark brown '70s-styled uniform.

I sold paintings periodically and supplemented my income by occasionally dealing drugs and photographing weddings. I was restless; in and out of relationships; traveled randomly; was frequently unemployed; and homeless for a short time in both L. A. and San Francisco before finally crash-landing back on my home turf at age thirty-three with a heart attack. I guess it would be an understatement to say it's been a fairly eventful life; even more, a life that I later realized troubled my parents to no end.

I was fortunate. Through all my mishaps and missteps, I was always aware of someone or something more that mattered. So I eventually cleaned up. Stopped doping and dealing. Quietly walked away from an assortment of characters and friends I had known since childhood. I gave up wanting to be right, read everything, learned gratitude and embraced my inner boy. I began to laugh more loudly and not take myself or others too seriously.

My writing deepened along with my thinking, and my painting grew more colorful and challenging. My photographs began to speak for the people they reposed in silver, and my capacity for empathy and love began to take on larger bounds. To this day I have not looked back.

What I have come to realize about myself these days is that I'm a pretty clear thinker (give or take a THC overloaded brain cell or two), but even more: I trust my thinking (believe me, there's nothing more debilitating than not being able to trust your own thinking, regardless of what others think). This may have never come about if I hadn't been so independent and introverted as a child growing up in a family of seven.

*   *   *

So, what makes one a pretty clear thinker? Being able to suspend judgment—to look at things lucidly, then proffer a conclusion without any bias attached. It's not an easy thing to do, but it's doable.

*   *   *

The snow finally came today (after stubbornly denying everyone a white Christmas). The sky opened up and suddenly gave way to a steady rain of flakes that slowly clothed the bare tree branches, and pulled a down-filled blanket across

The desolate morning landscape. By the time it was all over, it had covered the world in a twelve-inch quilt of shifting ivory; closing schools and buses, halting traffic—bringing an unexpected reprieve to the daily grind of living.

Looking out my window at the freshly fallen snow, I pondered how unpredictable life really is. It's been said that "we make plans...and God laughs." Well, not wanting to provide Him with too many comedic moments, I've decided to just free-fall into the oncoming year.

So much of my life has been "upturned" in the last ten months: the death of my father and the loss of job and friendships; the falling away of old habits and antiquated ways of thinking; the welcome embrace of the unknown and mystery. There's a capriciousness to life...both troubling and exhilarating.

*"Change is the law of life. And those who look only to the past or present are certain to miss the future."*
*-John F. Kennedy*

# JANUARY

## S M T W T F S

Last night the sky flashed and reverberated with the sights and sounds of exploding fireworks and blaring horns...a New Year coming into its own. As I sat in the darkness with the lights low, the music soft and a cold, winter rain tapping at my window, I mused about life and the year to come.

* * *

I was born on the last day in the first month of a new year. The year was nineteen fifty-three. My mother used to tell me stories about the moment I first came into the world and into the arms of my father. How he gathered me up from the hands of the midwife and cradled me in that same unsure manner he would often handle her best china. She knew those arms well—having been courted by them when she was just a teenager in high school, and comforted by them years later when her mother passed quietly away with cancer

My mother came from kettle-black, colored stock—or what was considered in most Negro circles as blue/black...skin so dark that one could almost detect subtle hues of violet in it. The old folks called it African-black, and swore it was a bloodline lest tainted by rape and miscegenation. Whatever—when my mother was eighteen, she was voted the prettiest girl in her graduating class.

My father's mother was bonafide full-blooded Kickapoo Indian; whose people had migrated out of southern Michigan into Oklahoma in the mid- 1980's. My father's father, like many blacks from the South, was the son of a Georgian sharecropper. I never really knew how the two of them met, but their union produced seven children of which two were girls. My father was their fourth child.

What most people remember right off about my father was his smoothed back, straight black hair, as jet as my mother's complexion...and his skin, which favored the color of dried orange peelings.

What I remember most about my father were his hands. He had huge, meaty hands. My earliest memories of being tossed in the air and netted by those hands are probably the reasons I am so self-assured today. And what child wouldn't feel assured held in the history of those thick, rugged hands.

*　　　　　　　　*　　　　　　　　*

From humble beginnings we are partnered with providence—given life through a particular woman who fell in love with a particular man; with histories both similar and distinct. That I was born from the union of these two disparate personalities is representative of what the German writer and poet Hermann Hesse once articulated as the "unique, the very special and always significant and remarkable point at which the world's phenomena intersects, only once in this way and never again."

From this unique coupling of DNA I was ushered into being; with the heart and spirit of both my parents. What they taught me was gleaned from the culture of their individual experiences...and what I learned from them came from the inscrutable discerning of my own fastidious personality.

*　　　　　　　　*　　　　　　　　*

I like to think that what I inherited from my mother was her quiet patience and humor, and a heart that tended to feel deeply about things. She was a woman who took great delight in her children, loved gardening and God (like most of her generation), and sang old jazz standards with uninhibited joy. Gloria Lynn, Carmen McRae, Ella Fitzgerald were some of my mother's favorites—singers who grace the shelves of my own personal music library.

She died way too young, and I wasn't able to develop the kind of relationship with her that I later had with my father—to be truthful, I never knew either of them intimately, that is, in the real sense of their aspirations and what their early childhood was like. It's easy to miss those opportunities while we're growing up. We view our parents as always having been grown and adult, but there was a time when they were other people's children...just like us.

My father was a Blues and jazz man, who loved Chuck Berry, B. B. King and Nat King Cole. My appreciation of Rhythm and Blues came from him; as did my creativity and my ability to do a multitude of things. With only a fifth-grade education he supported a family of seven kids, and was even able to send one off to college.

He loved reinventing things—like the time he installed gas burners beneath the top elements of our electric stove so that whenever the power went out during a really bad snowstorm, the family could still cook and keep warm.

He was also bent on improving our lot by moving us out of the colored neighborhood into the surrounding white neighborhood, where the homes were better. Our pets would be poisoned, the windows shattered, before we were finally driven back to the colored side of town. A few years later he would do it all over again.

What I gained from him wasn't any penchant for stubbornness, but one of perseverance, and a sense of rightfulness about what one deserves and is willing to go after. The schooling he gave me and my other brothers and sisters was set by example and went well beyond his own fifth-grade education.

*"The truth of it is, the first rudiments of education are given very indiscreetly by most parents."*
*-Richard Steel*

* * *

I miss my parents; who were married for more than fifty years. They had their moments, like many couples, but always supported each other. With her high school education my mother took charge of the paperwork while my father worked, often holding down two full-time jobs.

For a long time I was unaware that my father could barely read, having seen him in the early morning sitting and slowly flipping through our local newspaper. It was sometime later that my mother clued me into the fact that he was picking his way through with what words he knew or recognized, trying to glean some understanding of what had been written.

That's what always amazed me about the man: Regardless of the situation, he had little time for self-pity and doubt, and was constantly in the process of doing something—anything—in wanting to be better.

Of all the things that I inherited from his parenting, I think this one thing alone has made the biggest difference in my life and in my ability to weather the shifting storms of circumstance.

Living from your own place of authenticity leaves little time for regrets or for the failures of others in correlation to our happiness. Not only is it way too easy, but after a given amount of time, it's both irrelevant and nonproductive to continue to blame our past experiences and the compunctions of others for the current condition of our lives.

*　　　　　　　　　　*　　　　　　　　　　*

This morning while I was out running errands, I came upon a sign announcing a Martin Luther King Jr. holiday celebration scheduled on the property of a small, religious community college. I had to laugh, remembering when I was barely a teenager, how that same college wouldn't allow me or any other Black folks to even step on its campus grounds much less acknowledge our existence. But today it's a whole other story.

Sure, people change, but when you claim to be a source for what's good to go from God, well, I expect you to set a better example or at least take the lead in doing the just and right thing.

I think one of the reasons I no longer have an affiliation to any religious institution is the historical mistakenness of the white, evangelical Christian church, and how it always positioned itself on the wrong side of historical events: slavery, Jim Crow, the genocide of indigenous cultures and the Civil Rights Movement—just to name a few.

That it wasn't only the dupe, but also one of the main purveyors of White Supremacy, is something that it will no doubt have to take up with the Creator come the proverbial "Judgment Day," a reckoning that's sure to solicit a whole lot of nay saying.

*"When fascism comes to America, it will be wrapped in the flag and carrying the cross." - Sinclair Lewis*

*　　　　　　　　　　*　　　　　　　　　　*

So, today is the MLK Jr. holiday, and around the country there will be celebrations honoring the man and his message. Churches and schools will put on plays and present ceremonies, and his two most famous speeches—the 1963 March on Washington, "I Have a Dream" and the 1968 "Mountain Top" speech, delivered a year to the day before his assassination—will be replayed ad nauseam.

Don't get me wrong: I admire MLK, and when I was sixteen, I delivered a "King"-styled speech at such a commemoration—it's just that the constant pounding sound bites coupled with 50% off holiday sales commercials just seem to cheapen the message a bit.

It's sad that his most controversial speeches are seldom given much attention. Like the one he gave at NYC's Riverside Church, which, if we are honest, seems to reference several of the issues in the way the holiday is currently exploited.

Widely known as the speech that alienated both his parishioners and supporters, and rallied many of his distracters because of its opposition to the Vietnam War, his words were a prophetic refrain emblematic of where we find ourselves today as a society.

Standing behind a pew before an audience of his fellow clergymen, King proclaimed: "We must rapidly shift from a thing-oriented society to a person-oriented society. When machines and computers, profit motive and property rights are considered more important than people, the giant triplets of racism, materialism, and militarism are incapable of being conquered."

Truly ahead of his time, he echoed those words in the spring of 1967, nearly fifty years ago, when computer technology was in its infancy, and the glut of greed and materialism was merely hunger pain rumbling in the guts of many Americans.

Indeed, today, we live in not just a society, but a world that picks profit over people, and war over reconciliation.

* * *

It's funny how my Blackness just intrudes upon me. Like one day last week when I was sitting with a white co-worker and he started telling me about his family's accomplishments. How his father spent thirty years in the military and then came out and got a job at DuPont, where he labored for another thirty years—and how when he passed he left his mother pretty well-off. And he had invested in a lot of acreage near Branson, and how his family had a nice-size cabin that he and his other brother and sister frequented as a getaway in the summer. And there was nothing like fishing off the docks and watching the sun set on a crisp autumn night.

Settling back to look at me with steely blue eyes from beneath a bushy brow and an even bushier gray, full-bearded face, he finished: *"Yep, me and my folks have done pretty good."*

I was tempted to say, *"When he was nine, my father and his family were burned out of their house and home by the Klan."* But to be honest, that simply wouldn't have added anything positive to the conversation.

*  *  *

This intrusion of my Blackness is such a strange thing—it's like buying a particular model car, and for the first time noticing similar models swirling all around you. Like today, on the morning news, just before I was about to go off to work, I switched on the TV to catch the forecast, and there was this story about a former university football player who had just survived wrecking his car only to be shot dead by police. He was Black.

The incident, as reported by the Associated Press, described how the young man had wrecked his vehicle in the early a.m. just outside a small suburban community in North Carolina and, after freeing himself, sought help at the nearest home. The resident, startled by the loud banging on the door, quickly called police who, responding to a report of breaking and entering, encountered the twenty-four-year-old running toward them on a side road. He was "tasered" but eventually ended up being shot ten times...dying at the scene. The question posed by the local chapter of the NAACP: whether race played a role in the shooting of a black man by a white officer. Duh.

In his post-election book, *Between Barack and a Hard Place*, author Tim Wise insightfully articulates that the election of our first Black president could prematurely usher in the notion of a post-racial society. Subtitled *racism and white denial in the age of Obama*, Mr. Wise speculates that, despite evidence to the contrary, many Whites might jump to that conclusion, especially in a country long weary of its racist history.

At first glance, one would think that a concept only White people might adhere to; but for Black folks, who want nothing more than to move beyond the impediment of race, such a perception can have deadly consequence. And as a Black man I find it hard not to blame the victim in this case, knowing full well that the subtleties of racism are intricately woven into the fabric of American society—like fingerprints left at the scene months before the crime was ever committed. You don't actually have to be something in order to be influenced by the nuance of what it is, and even the most reasonable of those among us fall prey to the casual insidiousness of it all.

Innocence is the real victim here; that even in a state of trauma or shock,

Black folks must keep their wits about them in order to survive the vulgarity of bigoted stereotyping still prevalent in the world today. That one is constantly being viewed through a glass darkly (so to speak) obscuring even the most mundane circumstance, and setting the stage for events that, if we're honest, should never happen.

*  *  *

Being black informs nearly every aspect of my life. That's so sad, because it really shouldn't be that way. One should be able to go about everyday living without the intrusion of race: to shop and not be followed, to procure a loan without being financially maligned, to dine out and be served up front and accordingly, to get lost or have an accident, and not end up on a cold steel tray at the county morgue.

I don't think many white people really understand the nuances of institutional racism (it's such an indiscernible thing when viewed as being natural), nor do they ever seem to make a distinction between our dissimilar historical narratives.

*  *  *

It's easy to forget that the reality of others might be different from our own, especially in regards to race, gender or class—and it's such a maligned forgetfulness. To pretend that opportunities in education, home ownership and career choices were fair and across the board is a peculiar and selective kind of memory loss and one that errs easily on the side of revisionist attitudes and made-up rationalizations.

It's easy to think of history as fiction…I understand that. Because rape, lynching—the abuse and violation of another human being—can be such an unbelievable thing, and the memory of such events might seem subjective. However, their reality is undeniably non-fiction: men were lynched, burned at the stake; women raped and hung, their pregnant bodies ripped open and the fetus trampled. The pure evil of our humanity stands revealed for all to see and we become ashamed of that history, purposely turning our face from it.

So, like a child fearful of being punished, we reinvent the story, tell the tale, soften the blow, qualify it with words that twist and minimize our involvement or its importance, and sometimes we just outright lie about it.

It's such a sad narrative, this thing, this American dream we believe in.

*"There are some people that if they don't know, you can't tell 'em."*
*- Louis Armstrong*

* * *

There is this moment in the morning, when the sun comes up, and it hits the shades of my partially closed living room blinds, and the room is suddenly engulfed in a soft, warm, summer glow of golden/yellow. It's a soothing essence of color and light that blushes with brilliant intensity, then slowly fades as the sun inches up away from the horizon.

It makes me pause, and all the worry and list of things to be done—the laundry, the emails and the phone calls—whatever I'm doing can just wait, because there's a calmness radiated in that moment…a respite that is not commonly accessible.

No matter the season, though the time may be different…there is always that moment…when the sun strikes the blinds just right…and I am swept away by the wonder of it all.

* * *

Today, I celebrate my sixty-second birthday.

Who knew I would find myself having never married or had children. However, I came to terms with all that at fifty, reconciling the fact that it wasn't going to happen unless I could somehow persuade some young thirty-something to fall madly in love with me, to sacrifice both her body and nine months of her youth as an incubator for my seed and ego.

Well, that not gonna happen.

Life never turns out the way we expect it. But I'm all right with that. It's not like I didn't have a say in a lot of it. I mean, really, no one gets married by accident; nor do they unknowingly choose to have sex without realizing the possible consequences. I get that.

Still, looking back from sixty-two at my experiences and learning…I think I would have been an awesome father.

*"It is much easier to become a father than to be one."-Ken Nerburn*

# February

S M T W T F S

About a mile or so from where I live there is a nature park; a little over three hundred acres of natural, prairie grasslands and woods. The majority of the trails there are foot-worn and ragged, and there are even places where you have to cross the creek by stepping on stones that protrude just above the water line.

In the middle of summer, after the spring rains, the foliage is so lush and tangled that you find yourself cooled just from the humidity held hostage beneath its thick canopy of leaves. It's an awesome place.

It's a different kind of place in the winter. Sometimes I think a more honest place than in any other season. I hiked it today after another heavy snow; saw those same trees stripped of their plumage and clothed in gowns of white. Separate and unadorned, their branches clutching fitfully at the winter sky.

I've also hiked it in the aftermath of some of our famous Kansas "ice storms"... naked branches covered in crystal and dripping with the frozen tears of winter. They say to know nature is to know oneself. I do believe this to be true.

* * *

This snow today is relentless. Starting out Black History month with nothing but white around me—how ironic is that?

* * *

Recently, a good friend, who is White, asked me the significance of "Black History Month," being of the opinion that he considered all of us to be Americans who share a common history. He also questioned the use of the term "African-American," again citing the same reason.

Sometimes it's hard to explain the duality that W. E.B. Du Bois wrote about in *The Souls of Black Folks*, way back at the turn of the century—that "double consciousness" which seems to plague Black people even to this day. Of course, it was Carter G. Woodson who first established Black History Week; understanding the significance of history on the psyche of a people, especially those who are oppressed and buy into the trappings of that kind of thinking.

It's been said that original identity is land-based, that is, where our ancestors come from. Here, in these modern times, we can all trace our people back to a particular place and time. Whether they arrived eagerly by boat through the portal of Ellis Island in New York; or off the coast of Northern California across the threshold of Angel Island, enslaved and shipped like packaged goods across oceans of amber waves or stealthfuly crossing imaginary desert borders—the essence of who we are is eternally tied to a place of people and culture.

The title African-American was one that we, Black people, took upon ourselves, after all the demeaning monikers given to us (negro, colored, jigaboo, etc.)—it honors both our heritage (where we come from) and our history (where we've been), and is the clearest definition of who we are. To be real, Black folks have always lived hyphenated lives, most often viewing themselves through the eyes and histories of the dominant culture—which has never been very flattering.

In his autobiography, *The Measure of a Man*, actor Sidney Poitier credits his unyielding sense of self to his childhood on poverty-stricken Cat Island, where the human stain of blackness carried no evidence of inferiority and degradation. Lacking the burden of feeling flawed, and consistent exposures to the capabilities of people who looked like him, gently embedded in his personality a quiet sense of

Confidence; one devoid of suspicion and inadequacy concerning his abilities based solely on the color of his skin. Here in America, that was so not the case.

Redefining the attributes of who we are was necessary for us to do in order to understand both ourselves and our children. Laying down a foundation in her book *All About Love*, cultural critic Bell Hooks writes: "Definitions are vital starting points for the imagination. What we cannot imagine cannot come into being. A good definition marks our starting point and lets us know where we want to end up."

And where do we want to end up? As whole people capable of defining our lives.

* * *

I have a hard time with Black History Month. Not because I don't think it's necessary, but because it seems to stir up so many disparate emotions in me.

All those revelations about Black folks and their contribution to the development of the country, alongside the terror they had to endure, are simply unsettling.

*"Talking to black people reminds me of how black people have endured. Talking to white people reminds me of what black people have endured."*
*–Quentin Lucas*

It's sort of like watching "Roots." Contrary to popular belief, when "Roots" first appeared on the small screen back in the mid-'70s, most of the Black folks I knew weren't that keen on watching it. The Civil Rights Movement was just beginning its wane (even though there was still so much to be done), and the long record of discrimination and denial was finally being addressed—the last thing that many of us wanted to see was a replay of White Supremacy, the wounds of which at the time were still pretty fresh. We were more interested in looking forward instead of looking back.

Still, it was all good. "Roots" exposed White folks to the horrors of a history that was readily skipped over in textbooks—the same purpose that Black History Month continues to serve today. In the '70s we called history "His'-story"; what we know now is that his' story wasn't our story...and the revealing and retelling of that hidden truth was crucial for the healing of a people.

That we keep revisiting this slave narrative in movies like *Django Unchained* and the more credible *12 Years a Slave,* is an indication of our ambivalence with that history and how it has never been truly reconciled. The wounds of racism cut deep, historical lies maim and disfigure, and stereotypes reinforce our self-imposed differences. There's an arrogance in some white people that isn't easily forgiven. It comes from a casualness in the things they say and believe from their position of privilege. Only those among them who are the most sincere and conscious understand and recognize this, and those seem so few.

But let's be honest—most people, white, black or otherwise, have very little understanding of history...or their place in it.

* * *

Our common humanity transcends our preconceived differences.

* * *

A lot of history is historical. But America's racial history is in constant play and left in the hands of the dominant society. I know that's hard for some people to accept, because power can convey itself in many ways—by wealth, by force of arms, by sheer weight of numbers—but the elimination of hate and attitudes that disparage others lies chiefly in the hands of the governing group. Black History, therefore, isn't a static thing. Although it's acknowledged in the month of February, the incidents that make up that history are scattered throughout the year. Even today, small happenings of discrimination and hate continue to exert themselves in both words and actions so that this history, this American history, is in constant flux.

Our race and ethnicity are a big part of who we are, especially in the context of our world histories. There's no denying White Privilege; there's no denying a Middle Passage, a Trail of Tears, a Holocaust—horrific incidents in time and place that stole from people both their land and their humanity and any promise of a better future.

To deny any one of these events is a blasphemy to the audacity of each enduring spirit that sought to rise above the chaos of hate and inhumanity. To take ownership of one's place in the grand scheme of things, whether by actuality or inheritance, is to acknowledge that there was a wrong perpetrated, and the essence of that wrong still reverberates and affects us on myriad levels.

* * *

Another hard truth, especially when it comes to the subject of fairness, is that there has never been the equivalent of a Frederick Douglass or a Martin Luther King Jr. (apart from John Brown) to rise up out of the larger white community to take charge of justice. And I mean that in the sense of champion causes against both racial and social inequalities. Not since the War for Independence has anyone ever stepped forward to lead a movement that would truly endanger their personal life.

I find that telling. Perhaps things aren't dire enough to constitute such a challenge. I tend to believe that, if a messiah were ever to return again—regardless of how often he's been portrayed—I doubt if he would rise up from out of the dominant community.

* * *

Reading over my previous entry, I thought it pretty harsh, but then considered otherwise. The simple truth is usually hard, in that it challenges us on the complexities of being human. And being a good human being is hard work. It requires sacrifice and a willingness to be wrong about a lot of things we think we know.

This much I do know: My struggles with my blackness are a part of my struggle with being human. If I stand outside the stereotypes forced upon me by the external world, I stand within the context of my humanness and all its strengths and failings. I find that I'm no more or less than anyone else; that I'm just as perfectly flawed as the next person.

But you know what? I can work with that.

*"Not one drop of my self-worth depends on your acceptance of me."*
*-Quincy Jones*

*　　　　*　　　　*

Race and the color of my skin will continue to define me, as long as I live in a world that continues to define people based upon their outward appearances. But that's okay; I know and understand that I'm more than what my skin dictates; I'm the results of all the people I've ever met, and that diversity of people makes me more than what my appearance says. It makes me, I believe, a better man.

*　　　　*　　　　*

I grew up a member of the African Methodist Episcopal (A. M. E.) Church, which was founded by Minister and activist Richard Allen in the early 1600 s and was the first established national Black church in the country.

I taught Sunday school and for a long time thought I might become a minister myself. But all that changed the more I studied and learned about the distortions in both the biblical and historical scholarship being fed to me.

God is such an abstract concept—and believing in God, even more so. We're taught to believe that it's a given, that it's supposed to be in a certain way that defines the truth. But that's far from true. Religion is mostly dogma, a creation in the same way the concept of time was created. And just like time, it aids in setting the parameters that frame our lives.

Faith is dichotomous, just like being human, but not so much it seems with religion. Some people believe that God (in a scriptural sense) no longer inserts Himself into the affairs of men (whether personal or on a secular level)—if that's true, then what good is prayer or believing?

Still others deem God to be beneficent creditor and see prayer as discretionary spending. They're always asking to be delivered from or having something delivered to them.

The truth is, we're all novices when it comes to the work of living, but what seasons us and makes us more is our willingness to engage faith on all its levels of intricacy: in matters of the heart, in realms of the secular, and in our relationship to the divine and how it permeate our lives.

It took a long time before I understood that the dogmatism of religion can be a very unhealthy thing; capable of blocking the true blessings of a just and benevolent Spirit.

* * *

Growing up in the Black church back then was a very edifying experience, unlike today, with its mega churches mimicking its segregated evangelical counterpart and its small neighborhood churches filled with aging single women and their children.

Forced by segregated times, the five dissimilar houses of faith that bordered my community were markedly interwoven, and shared the vocal and inspirational talent of their congregations. Both ministers and parishioners moved in and out of each other's traditions, collectively providing sustenance for a people constantly under heel.

Back then, my four brothers and I were known as *Benny's Boys* (after our father), who harmonized on such familiar tunes as, "I Shall Not Be Moved," "This Little Light of Mine" and "Woman at the Well"—each accompanied by our father on harmonica. One of our most popular performances (coming near the end of our career as we were outgrowing the experience) was a rendition of the Curtis Mayfield classic "People Get Ready"—the only time we were not accompanied by our father, but by a young brother from the neighborhood who played the electric guitar (something unheard of in the church at that time). Needless to say…we were a big hit!

* * *

I had to relearn my spirituality (as opposed to religion), which happened back in the early '80s, during what was then being referred to as the second "Harlem Renaissance," a second go-round of significant cultural awareness in my parent community.

The historical revelations of Egyptologist Dr. Ben-Jochannan, the psychological underpinnings of Dr. Wade Nobles and Dr. Na'im Akbar—all coming from an Afrocentric prospective—literally saved my life and changed the way I approached analyzing myself and those most like me.

I discovered that understanding myself on a historical level led to understanding myself on a spiritual level, which, in turn, revealed its truth to me on a personal level. That the personal is also the most universal is an unacknowledged given. In the end, we're all simply human beings in different skin and gender clothing, trying to understand our place in the world.

* * *

I came of age in the '50s, in the rural Midwest, black and poor and somewhat oblivious to the dysfunction of the world around me. As a child between the ages of seven and twelve, there was a lot I didn't understand about racism, poverty and my place in the planet. This was due in large part to the discerning of my parents, who always managed to manipulate circumstance to their favor.

Without shielding me or my other brothers and sisters from the harsh reality of the times (we were well-aware of what it meant to be black and the dangers it afforded), they provided us with the health of a well-nurtured home life—one filled with familiar rituals and habits, devoid of fear, worry, and the nightmare world of social injustice lurking just outside our living room door.

They were aware of how important normalcy was to our sense of growth as whole human beings. And because of that, my early boyhood development was one of unrivaled joy, filled with raucous boyhood play, and instrumental in the kind of person I am today. Looking back, I realize how fortunate I was to have such loving and discerning parents—to say that they helped define me is truly an understatement. In that sense I was pretty lucky.

*"For salvation and redemption one must frame one's own questions, seek one's own answers, in the boundary of one's own time. Each generation must be responsible for itself, and there's no escaping that."*
*—Sidney Poitier*

*"It was such a spring day as breathes into a man an ineffable yearning."*
*- John Galsworthy*

# March

## S M T W T F S

It's early and still dark—headlights glare, reflecting sparkles splashing off of roadside puddles. Buses roll up to the curb of the grade school across the street, and even in the rain, I can hear the laughter of children—the hustle of hurried feet scurrying across wet pavement. The world outside my window is alive and well.

* * *

For a long time I suffered from a lack of believing in myself. It wasn't until I was in my mid-forties that I was finally able to trace it back to a particular time and place; when the seeds of disenchantment were first sown…taking root in the fertile soil of myth, and vigilantly cultivated by the edicts of a dysfunctional society.

In seeking out this understanding, two separate but distinct incidents return to memory—both taking place in grade school and both, in large ways, having to do with race and the color of my skin.

The first happened when I was about nine; in front of my third-grade classroom. At the time there was a popular hair cream commercial (catch phrase: "A little dab will do you") featuring a woman running her hand easily through some guy's hair. The teacher, for whatever reason, chose to put me in line with several other boys: blond, wavy hair, blue-eyed and rosy-cheeked—and little ol' me. Dark and nappy-headed. She proceeded to have the girls go up and run their fingers through the boys' hair. I remember standing there feeling somewhat bewildered and embarrassed as none of them even attempted to do so with me. Obviously some cruel joke perpetrated at my expense?

The second occurrence was more dark and ominous—a blatant expression of White Supremacy—as a little white girl told me that she could have me hanged for touching her. I woke up for days after that, from nightmare images of myself hanging from one of several large oaks that shaded the playground yard.

They say that memory is fiction. That time has a way of embellishing things, making them more if not less of what they truly are. But for a child, whose ability to discern is limited, every incident of abuse registers and informs their understanding of themselves and the world in which they live. Like the head of a tick burrowed under the skin, it contaminates the psyche, and if left untreated, continues to fester and infect, doing irreparable harm.

Exhuming and re-examining these two contrasting events was a salve for my spirit. Tracing the lineage of my injured esteem back to those school-yard-days of growing up under the curse and distain of my blackness was both liberating and necessary.

*"Be careful how you are talking to yourself,*
*because you are listening."*
*--Lisa Hayes*

* * *

The things that happen in our lives are sometimes good and sometimes bad, and sometimes they're simply the things that happen. We give them meaning by how we interpret them. Suspending judgment is crucial because doing so allows us to move on, but that's so hard to do when nearly all our thoughts are judgment calls.

There are roads we travel based upon our temperament and the circumstances of the life into which we are born. Race, gender, sexual identity and a whole bunch of other things play their part, as well as whether we are born into wealth or poverty; or into a first, second, or third-world perspective.

None of this can ever be discounted. But, there comes a point where we must reassess the opinions we unintentionally have developed about ourselves—that crossroad where it's all too easy to get lost. We simply forget that those circumstances and our personal histories are only a part of our definition. They don't completely define us.

There's no getting around a troubled sense of self-esteem. Just to be born human is to inherit a thousand hurts and failings, each one cutting away at our sense of wholeness. Overcoming the hurts of the past is a challenge that has to be confronted, or it will continue to influence our interactions with others and with ourselves. This I have experienced firsthand.

* * *

I read somewhere that the word *educate*, at its root, means "to draw out," that the essence of intellect is already there waiting to be coaxed into being. And like the statue residing at the heart of the stone is dependent on the skill of the sculptor to release its image, so too is the aptitude of the student dependent on the skill of the teacher "to draw out" the best in him/her.

Why do I know this to be true? I wasn't a good student. At best I was average and borderline failing. But all it took was one, good teacher who saw beyond the gruff exterior and surly attitude to recognize the vast potential that resided within me—to change my life forever.

* * *

So this is where I'm forced to defer when it comes to race—because I wasn't as fortunate as some folk who attended all-black schools where the teachers as well as the material looked like and involved them. I went to an integrated high school, and both of the teachers who influenced me were white.

The first was my tenth-grade art teacher, Mrs. Mayo, who, after praising my ability to sketch and draw, encouraged me to sketch and draw people who looked like me. As strange as that sounds, I had never once thought or considered doing that. I learned to draw from comic books, and at that time all the superheroes were white, so I drew what I knew and saw. This is my own personal testimony to the subtle indoctrinations and issues of esteem directly related to popular images and the dominant culture.

The second teacher was Mrs. Hoffman, my junior year creative writing teacher. Not only did she sign my yearbook, *"To one of the most talented students I've ever had,"* but later she went on to pen a poem about me that ended up being published in a small literary collection. She believed in my writing ability long before I did.

Along the way there were individual friendships from all the many white people who accepted me for who I was—in defiance to the times and family relations. They understood and never dismissed my reality by saying, *"When I look at you I don't see the color of your skin."* They saw the color of my skin and more: the history that went with it and their place in that history. They were honest and open relationships that allowed me to be angry, but also allowed me to express my love and appreciation for who they were as distinct individuals.

*                    *                    *

I've been thinking about something that abolitionist Frederick Douglass once said: "*It is easier to build strong children than to repair broken men.*" The repair of broken men is nearly impossible; in so much that we are such a broken society. It's hard to learn if we're wounded and even harder for the wounded to learn from us. But this is what I know about good teachers and good people in general: They change us.

The value of a good teacher lies not only in the teaching of the moment, but in the learning that comes after. When the student, who was once ignored and marginalized, upon graduating continued to read and write and explore the larger world—simply because he was taught to see his fuller self.

It's been said that whenever we have a conversation with someone, a part of us is left with them; whether we're in agreement or not, the essence of the content registers on minute levels that are impossible to discern. That's why it's so important to speak truth to power in ways that edify and inform the spirit. We're too fragile a species to do otherwise. Thoughtlessness can wound us. Insensitivity can bleed us like a knife. Indifference can break our hearts, leaving us feeling disconnected and lost.

*                    *                    *

I'm more full of myself than I've ever been. But the difference between confidence and conceit is a huge one. In Jamaica they have an expression concerning smugness. They say, "You be smellin' yourself," which sounds pretty accurate about me.

In his most recent tome, *Confidence:* overcoming low self-esteem, insecurity, and self-doubt, personality profiler Tomas Chamorro-Premuzic, alludes to confidence as merely a façade, and that most displays were simply boisterous attempts at putting one's insecurities in a superior light. He concludes that competence is the best purveyor of confidence, and the more capable one was, the more confident they became.

I can attest to that. Confidence was such a hard-won attribute for me. And it continues to be a struggle at times. I must say, though, I take great pride in having overcome some of the obstacles I've encountered on this journey through life, but being human makes it a war of ongoing small battles—some won, some lost.

These days..."I be smellin' myself just fine, thank you."

*And he said: "You pretty full of yourself ain't chu." So she replied: "Show me someone not full of Herself and I'll show you a hungry person."*
*-Nikki Giovanni*

*    *    *

I'm both affected and infected by the attitudes and ways of the people around me. And I think this is probably true of all of us. That regardless of ethnicity, sex, class or gender orientation, the fact that we're more alike than unalike links us to that undeniable likeness of being human and all its inherited failings.

Our commonalities are the same things that make us special and unique—the ultimate paradox—they distinguish us from one another while at the same time acknowledging our similarities and the fact that we're simply the same persons dressed up in different color and gender costumes.

*    *    *

Double standards always come into play whenever we believe we're better or more entitled than someone else based upon perceived differences. Denial of another's individual humanity simply because they were born of different parentage is both fundamentally wrong and immoral. We'll always have more in common with each other than with any other kind of life on the planet.

Don't get me wrong. I believe all sentient life is of value, but if you would rather be stranded on a deserted island with the family pet instead of another human being—well, I think they have a word for that.

*    *    *

I used to think that bigotry was fast losing its legs on the tracks of modern living. I used to believe if we could simply let go of all the old, false and fearful ways of thinking, then we might possibly begin to be in this world on a whole other level in appreciation of our diversity.

I'm not so sure anymore.

Confronting the flawed realities of the past isn't an easy thing. No one wants to give up their position on the ladder of hierarchy for fear of meeting those same people on the way down whom they climbed over on the way up. Still, no matter how much some might protest, in their hearts they knew the deck was unevenly stacked, and the fear of reprisal (that they might be treated in the same manner) is at least a sincere, paranoid response.

But let's be honest. That hasn't been the demonstrative response of oppressed minorities in this country. They have seldom returned hatred in kind. That's why it's so hard for people of color to be told that they're racist. Their displays of anger and violence most times are in direct response to the discriminations levied against them by the dominant society.

Bigotry, in its clearest description, usually pertains to an attitude of narrow-mindedness in both thoughts and deeds, and particularly with regard to opinions that differ from those of our own. It seems few people today are really interested in understanding another's point of view, especially if it's in conflict with something they have long believed.

I'm always amazed at how people will accept the latest improvement on a thing or modus operandi based upon some recent discovery or science, but will stubbornly refuse to accept any illumination as it concerns biblical scholarship or history—a bigoted response, to be sure. However, I believe one way of overcoming both our personal and public bias is a simple respect for our commonalities.

* * *

Nothing stays the same, especially in the realm of the individual. And change is the only constant in our lives, but only if we allow it to be so.

It's been said that we're a most "privileged species" because we possess a nervous system that makes it possible to be conscious that we are conscious. And because of that ability we have the capacity to reason and grow and create. No other species on the planet has this distinction.

However, it seems because of this unique awareness, that we're also the most inconsiderate species on the planet; that our superior consciousness give us license to do whatever we please in regards to ourselves and other living things, and with little consideration for the consequences.

In acknowledging this place of "privilege," I appreciate that I'm in a perpetual state of growth and change. I'm constantly reviewing and renewing my commitment to understanding as well as evaluating the words and actions of those around me, and to do anything less is to constrict awareness and settle for a life of increasing stagnation. As writer Gail Sheehy puts it, "Changes are not only possible and predictable but to deny them is to be an accomplice to one's own unnecessary vegetation."

I like that.

*     *     *

Looking back, I realize that I have always reinvented myself, and each time in a more forward-moving direction. From introverted and awkward, solitary and brooding, alone and sorrowful, to extroverted and confident, friendly and hopeful, single and satisfied; to where I find myself today: sociable and competent, congenial and optimistic, distinct and somewhat contented at being able to handle life's myriad circumstances.

I am a born-again believer. I believe we live a thousand lives within this one lifetime—that every mistake we learn from and every hardship we overcome is a born-again experience. We die and are reborn in what we know and, hopefully, in what we begin to believe and accept about ourselves.

*"I think somehow we learn who we really are and then live with that decision." -Eleanor Roosevelt*

# April

## S M T W T F S

Yesterday, when the wind shifted and the clouds rolled in on a cool breath of air left over from winter, I decided to spend the day from the inside looking out. So I stayed inside and read most of the day, taking time out to watch an old black-and-white movie that I had stumbled across in the early afternoon. It was a good day.

Last night I went to bed early and had a pretty restful night. It was easy for me to fall asleep, and if I dreamed at all, they were peaceful dreams, because I can't remember the faintest hint of anything other. I haven't used an alarm clock now for over thirty years. These days I simply awaken to the natural rhythms of my body, or, if it's summer and the windows are left open throughout the night, to the sound of morning doves cooing at the rising sun.

I got up later than usual…about five-thirty or six. The house was cool and quiet.

I washed the sleep from my eyes; boiled water for tea; turned on the computer; opened the blinds. It's deep and dense outside…the darkness before the dawn. For the next hour I read, sipped tea, watched the sun yawn and stretch its arms across the sky outside my living room window. It's the thirteenth day of April… and there's not the slightest hint of spring being in the air.

* * *

It used to be that the transition from winter to spring was a slow and subtle event which revealed itself in sweeping thunderstorms and torrential rains—not so much these days. Whether one believes in global warming or not, something elemental in our weather has changed and the seasons are no longer as predictable as they once were.

I miss that…the change of easily defined seasons—when spring was readily identified by its cool sudden showers and thundering lightning storms, and summer by the sweltering heat of its long yellow days. I miss an autumn that transcribes itself with Technicolor bursts of red and orange and yellow trees dappling the countryside, and winters so snowy and cold that having a "white Christmas" was a given.

I miss nature distinctly revealed.

* * *

Several years ago I lost my job. It was the worst time ever to be unemployed. With the economy on life support and hemorrhaging jobs from having been gutted by the corporate sector, whole families and lifestyles were bleeding profusely and on the verge of being wiped out. That I was wrongfully terminated mattered little to the powers that be, which is usually the case; few corporate entities are known for their sensitivity in regards to the ramifications of the decisions they make, especially in these troubled times.

What that experience taught me, however, was twofold: that both people and institutions are seldom what they claim to be, but rather façades of the bottom-line principles they often represent. And regardless of their intent, whenever these people or institutions reveal to us their true nature, they free us from the chains we tether to them that detached us from ourselves.

That single, unexpected turn of events, once again, led to the serendipitous understanding that whatever happens in our lives, whether by intention or contentious circumstance, puts us squarely at the heart of where we find ourselves today. Whether right or wrong, every act or inaction, every failure and every success, influences our thinking and affects our attitude and opinion regarding the choices we make—and with each decision the course of our lives is forever altered.

The road less traveled has always led me to a place both unfamiliar and brimming with incredible possibilities, but so too, has the road most traveled. There's a bizarre order to the randomness of how the universe works. Things are always happening just when they need to happen, and when I pay attention, I begin to notice this happening all the time. Still, instrumental in all those arbitrary starts and stops are the things I do and say that take me in a decided direction. This is how life changes us, and this is how we change our lives.

*　　　　*　　　　*

When we're aware, we're always present in the infinite possibilities of the next moment.

Every day we choose to live within the context of the life we've created for ourselves. And every day we casually go about defining it based upon all the things we do and say and how we interact with the world and those around me.

What I know now is that we all have "history," which shouldn't be confused with "baggage." That history is the story of our life experiences comprising all the people, things and events that have happened to us from as far back as we can strain our minds to remember.

If I look back at that history with eyes of awareness, it becomes the stuff of lessons learned; the twenty-twenty vision of hindsight. But if I take that history and carry it with me, it's transformed. That's when it becomes baggage. And all the lessons of the past; all the misery and slights, wrongs and judgments, all the litter of unresolved issues become pack and parcels of the load I carry into the space of each new, separate and distinct encounter. It infects them; takes away their uniqueness by imposing the failures of the past onto the possibilities of the present to the benefit of no one.

The history of my life is often buried beneath the lies I tell myself, and I must take ownership for my part in the telling. In a world that has little problem with pounding the spirit out of my dreams and desires, I've often joined in on the madness: cursing myself for my failings, hating myself for my appearance, loathing myself for the things I bought into back in the day when I was young and hardly knew any better.

Like the skin on an onion, as I grow older, I start to peel away those layers that have begun to mold and stink of half-truths. I cry for the person I never was—the person I wanted to be and the person I have become. This is important because the betrayal was from my own thinking and a flawed worldview of how things were supposed to be.

Now, to uncover the truth of who I really am, I need only come clean to the deception perpetrated against myself, and review that history in order to sift through and unload the baggage that burdens me on this journey toward reconciliation.

* * *

Yesterday, my sister called to tell me that my uncle was dying. One of my mother's three surviving brothers, he was a backdoor neighbor (along with a half-dozen or so other relatives) who occupied an eight-block area that framed the colored section of the town where I grew up.

Once, when the downtown TG&Y store caught fire, I remember him soaked to the skin and smiling wildly as he helped the firemen wrestle with the hoses in their attempt to extinguish the blaze. And for nearly twenty years he worked alongside my father as a janitor at the county courthouse.

My uncle was a small, springy man with soft brown hound dog eyes, and an excited, stuttering laugh. He loved gardening, and every spring would dig his plot by hand with pitchfork and spade where he planted collar, turnip and mustard greens, tomatoes and onions—especially onions, which he'd yank fresh from the soil. Polishing the dirt off on his trousers, he'd chomp into those onions as if they were God's little green apples.

Running around with my uncle was always big fun. The most mischievous of my mother's brothers (one would later become the first African American police officer in the county), he'd take my cousins and me for daybreak raids on the large commercial cornfields bordering town. We'd sit on the hood of his car as he slowly cruised up and down the graveled roads, then took turns leaping off and filling our gunnysacks with the plumpest and most ripe ears. He did have a thing for drinking, though…which probably lead to his current state of un-health.

My sisters are coming into town this Friday; so we plan to visit him under hospice care at my cousin's house. Not looking forward to that.

* * *

Thinking about my uncle has brought up memories of the day my father passed.

I got the call from my sister early that morning, just as I was about to go off to work, informing me that he had taken a bad turn during the night and was rushed by ambulance to the hospital.

I remember thinking and praying on my way down that I would get there in time enough to possibly speak with him. He had been so frail and ailing since my last visit—a shell of the man who could wrestle all five of us boys to the ground in roughhouse play, and pulled engines from cars by hand and chain.

For nearly twenty years he worked two full-time jobs to support our family of seven. Rising early to work at Cowley's lumber yard, unloading pallets of brick and timber, and planning rough cuts into standard width and length boards; breaking briefly in the afternoon for a quick supper before going off to work at the county Court House alongside my uncle and several other colored custodians employed there. He was not a large man, but rather stocky and stout, with huge muscular arms and hands like weathered baseball mitts.

Old age ambushed my father. I remember him once telling me about a time he was out with a much younger co-worker, and they were crossing a field going uphill, and how he couldn't keep up. In that instant he realized that he was no longer the young man he felt himself to be in his mind; that time had accosted him, and had quietly stolen the youthful virility that was so much a part of his person.

In her book *My Stroke of Insight*, neuroanatomist Jill Bolte Taylor explains that the reason we all feel this way is because the neurons in our brains never age; they remain in their same birth state—and so we are left with this internal feeling of youth at the age of thirty, sixty-five, and eighty-seven, that never changes even as our bodies do. It's a cruel deception perpetrated by a mind that can't help itself to know any differently. I know at sixty. I feel the very same way.

*                    *                    *

The realization that my father had aged had come to me some years earlier at the funeral of one of his contemporaries. We were sitting together during the ceremony when I happened to look over at him. In that moment it dawned on me that he had aged. He was still my father, but older; animated by the mannerisms that inevitably come with aging: the slack skin and deeply trenched brow, the slow-chew jaw movement often displayed in silence when no words are being spoken. The almond shape eyes of his Kickapoo ancestry and burnt orange cast of his skin…darker now and spotted. There was a short period, in his mid-sixties, when his straight, jet black hair turned a dirty blond just before going gray—ghostly Aboriginal.

On that morning, lying in the hospital bed, he was nothing like the man I had grown up with. It was as if time had slowly sucked the life out of him—literally—shrinking him down to nearly half his size and weight.

I took his hand and spoke to him softly; wanting him to know that I was there; he turned to me locking my eyes, and I remember thinking: What is he trying to say? In the unfathomable silence between us, I probed his face, looking to discern some hint of meaning.

He passed away later that morning—a message from my sister was waiting for me upon my arrival back home. And it was only later, during a quiet moment of

Reflection, that I finally realized the deep loss present in his eyes and face: the loss of education and opportunity, the loss of ideas and dreams, the loss of brothers and sisters who all preceded him in death, and the loss of my mother whom, in the end, he felt he had not done enough for.

It was the loss that came with being a Black man in America, at a time when America had little regard for black people.

*                    *                    *

It always comes back to race and the color of my skin. I try not to carry that history as baggage but there's really no way around it—and it's such an insidious thing for black people to deal with.

Attaching the sum of loss to the color of my father skin might appear to be a stretch, but to most black folks it's readily apparent. Sure, these are losses common to every man and woman, regardless of color, but it's the context that's different. Not having the real freedom to accomplish one's heart's desire based upon the circumstance of race is a reality not born to all people.

I'm not dismissing the damaging effects of being raised in a dysfunctional household, nor the psychological harm inherited from incidents of sexual abuse. Those things are just as reprehensible and wound our psyche in ways too numerous to mention —but institutional racism and discriminations that obstruct our humanity are a breed of their own—they snap at us like rabid dogs let loose and unchained, their bark every bit as vicious as the rip of their bite.

On a road trip several years before his death, my father told the story of a time when he was a young man just out of the service, and there was a car he wanted to buy; but the salesman said to him, "Boy, I ain't gonna sell you that car, because that car's too good for a colored man." I remember the questioning sound in his voice and the look of loss in his eyes at the utter incomprehensibleness of it all. "I had the money," he said lowly, in a tone swaddled in perplexity. "I don't know what it is that makes some white folks so mean."

Even as I write these words, a quiet sadness sweeps over me.

* * *

I think a lot of my father's loss and disappointments had sometimes later come to manifest themselves through me on a very subconscious level. I'm not sure if I can really explain it, but I think a lot of what my father had missed out on in life, I have, in some ways, been trying to make up for through my own personal accomplishments—and I wouldn't be the least bit surprised if there were other brothers out there who were attempting to do the same.

Well-educated and accomplished black men who one day looked over at their aging fathers with hearts full of honest and sincere regret; realizing how much they had sacrificed, as well as how much they had been cheated...denied their own opportunity, all because of the color of their skin and the times they happen to be born into.

Thinking about this today…I realize, again, how fortunate I am.

* * *

My father may not have understood, "What makes some white folks so mean," but I'm beginning to have a pretty good idea—because it's that meanness that always seems to be at the forefront of both personal and social progress for me and other persons of African descent.

When I look back at America's history, I can't help but be struck by the sheer intensity of cruelty perpetuated against people of color by white people. Don't get me wrong: All people can be cruel. Man's inhumanity against his fellow man is a well-documented historical fact on nearly every continent of the planet. But the cruelty built and perpetuated upon the theoretical foundation of White Supremacy is a whole other thing.

Canadian scholar Michael Bradley, in his 1990 controversial treatise, *The Iceman's Inheritance*, postulates that the evolution of European people under the harsh and hostile conditions of the Caucasus Mountains during the Wurm Ice Age had a profound impact on their psychological makeup. He theorized that the hyper vigilance involved in constantly pitting oneself against a hostile environment was particularly influential in the development of a more aggressive personality—making people of Caucasian descent more confrontational in their relationship to both the natural world and other people.

It's a pretty plausible explanation when you look back at their history, especially when encountering native people. Whether indigenous to the North American wilderness or the jungles of Africa and Brazil, the doctrine of Manifest Destiny—of expansion and domination solely for the purpose of profit and greed—was justified from a position of moral superiority based upon one physical characteristic: the color of another's skin.

It's a pretty hard sale, but in reality, one can justify anything if one is willing to tell a lie, and then corroborate that lie by manipulating circumstance. Hide the other's history, forbid their language and pass laws that claim they're just one step down on the ladder from being human.

The only problem with telling that kind of lie is that you have to keep proving it over and over to yourself in order to make it true, and one of the ways you do that is through complete denial of their humanity. That denial makes the other inhuman and different, and easily justifies aggression, especially if you're somewhat predisposed to that particular trait.

But maybe "predisposed" is too harsh a word? Maybe it's more of an inclination, which reveals itself more readily in acts of unparalleled violence against themselves as well as those who are different. The fact that ninety-nine percent of serial killers are white, and that the vast majority of high school mass shootings are perpetrated by disassociated white adolescents, seems to mirror Mr. Bradley's supposition.

Aggression is part of human nature—I get that—but one has to admit that there seems to be an over-the-top response in their opposition to a lot of things: white flight and suburban sprawl in opposition to integration, cries of reverse discrimination in opposition to affirmative action (regardless of the fact that they have forever been the beneficiaries of the status quo).

Writer Michael Kimmel in his book *Angry White Men*, calls it "aggrieved entitlement"—a sort of narcissistic response to the various oppositional situations they find themselves confronting these days.

Truth be told: I think believing the lie is hard on white people. We may bear the brunt of their misguided hate and anger, but being confronted by the reality that the other is not as inferior as you've been told, can be a pretty unforgiving shot to the ego. As any educated and well-spoken Black man can attest, coming into that situation is very telling.

*"Nothing is easy to the unwilling."-Nikki Giovanni*

I once worked with this white guy from South Dakota, who had very little, if any, close contact with people of color other than the Native Americans who populated the state—and even then, I quickly discerned, his interaction had been very limited.

From day one he felt the need to prove that what he thought he knew about me was true, and one of the ways he did that was in not sharing with me the necessary information needed to do my job. Not only would he withhold pertinent information, but he would become increasingly irritated if I used words that he had a hard time understanding.

I'm a writer, so words are sort of my first language. They spill over the full of my lips like water rushing over stones, clearing away the muck of stagnant thinking and slime of murky rationalizations. That I challenged my co-worker's belief on many levels was truly disturbing to him and revealed itself in all kinds of defensive behaviors: the defiant stance and crossed arms whenever we talked; the subtle smirk of "I don't believe a word you say," as he listened, and the constant challenge to any and all suggestions I offered.

Sure, you could say, I may have been reading more into it; that it just may have been his personality and the way he dealt with everyone. But come on, when nothing, and I mean nothing, one says is acceptable or valid in even the smallest sense, then one gets the feeling that there's something more afoot. Regardless, we all know when we're being disregarded.

Still, as hard as the lie of racial superiority is on white people, the opposing truth—that race matters in nearly every aspect of a Black person's life—is even more devastating. You find yourself constantly second-guessing the small

slights you might encounter in various situations; falling back on that familiar but notorious mantra... "is it because I'm black?" You wonder: Did I not get the job? Am I being ignored? Do they not like me?

You feel trapped between the possibility that you know, and the actuality that you don't know, but are forced to question given the reality of racism and its constant imposition on even your most casual encounters. It's an insidious paranoia that not only challenges right thinking, but can easily lead to crippling cynicism, and a false sense of always feeling persecution.

It's hard to be at peace in the world, and with the world, when you find yourself continuously in that place—that limbo state of never knowing. But what I've discovered is that the surest way out of this hell, this insane personal predicament, is only through forgiveness. Something that a lot of black folks have always been aware of.

*"Black people have always been America's wilderness*
*in search of a promised land."*
*-Cornel West*

*     *     *

I guess I say forgiveness, becomes, forgiveness has very little to do with others and more to do with ourselves. As therapist Colin Tipping explains in his book *Radical Forgiveness*, the need to condemn others is dropped when we're willing to forgive. And that "victim consciousness," which he defines as the conviction that someone has done us wrong, and as a result, is responsible for our lack of peace and happiness, no longer takes center stage in our life.

When we suffer an injury or grievance and don't forgive, we initiate the beginnings of a long, hurtful courtship with both our pride and personal sense of betrayal. As we relive the wrongs, resentment and an unrelenting desire to even the score begin to slowly stoke the flame of our embittered heart—making peace with ourselves impossible. Left unresolved, these repressed emotions often leave us in an elevated state of anguish, yearning for retribution and release. To be unforgiving is to cultivate a mind-set of duplicity and self-abuse; to become both victim and perpetrator. This isn't a healthy place to be.

Forgiveness, however, is a choice. It's my "get out of jail free" card. Not only does it provide me with a gratifying sense of relief, but it puts my attention squarely back on the frontlines of the present—no longer chained to the wrongs and hurts of the past, I'm free to move on and get about the work of making my life happen. This is a good thing.

*                    *                    *

I forgive. But I can't forget, because my blackness is a dark spot on the rose-colored glasses of the larger white society. And until they remove those glasses, and begin to see more clearly the impact of their presence on those whom they consider inferior, then I'll continue to be forced to view the world and my place in it *"through a glass darkly."*

*"We cannot think of being acceptable to others until we have first proven acceptable to ourselves." -Malcolm X*

## May

S M T W T F S

This morning the air outside is cool and still. There is stillness to the start of the day that only Sunday possesses. Unlike the early-morning rush of Monday through Friday, and the errand-filled haste of Saturday, Sunday has a way of reclaiming its original intention…a way of bringing respite to the weariness that often accompanies living.

This morning, with the air clear and free of humidity, I sat on the back deck in the darkness and watched the sun slowly raise the blinds on the day around me. In the distance I could hear my neighbor's rooster crow, and the clock tower in the square chimed musically on the hour. I was tempted to take a walk to the square and sit quietly in the stone gazebo and watch the trains rumble through, their horns muted by city ordinance.

It's only on Sundays that silence grips the city so succulently.

*                    *                    *

Here, in my old-fashioned part of town, where alleyways cut a tic-tac-toe pattern between the houses, and playing children take shortcuts across adjoining lawns, we live a much less tethered life—a throwback of sorts to a much simpler time when neighbors talked over their fences, and appearances weren't taken so critically.

In our old suburban core, where crabgrass, clover and dandelions proliferate, we're able to express ourselves more individually. Unlike the more recently developed subdivisions, with their designer landscapes and homeowners associations barking out orders of what one can and can't do. The people here build play houses in huge, old-growth walnut trees that tower three stories high; plant massive vegetable gardens; and harbor a chicken or two in sturdy, well-made wire pens.

The homes that dapple the neighborhood are an eclectic blend. Restored Victorians with ornate trim painted in faint contrasting earth-tone hues, rub shoulder to shoulder with rustic brick and mortar Ranches and old New England-styled Cape Cods, each unique in their representation of our very diverse community.

Several large houses having fallen into neglect, were recently taken over by lawyers, restored and transformed into office space; while others, left abandoned and in various states of disrepair, were rescued by young entrepreneurs looking to invest in the city's emerging "original town" renewal efforts.

My house, bordered on one side by an alley that tees off parallel to the back yard, is a little over a hundred and sixteen years old. I was told by the inspector, who contorted his way into a very dark and foreboding crawlspace, that the joist cradling it was made of rough-hewed cedar beams that actually measure 4x12, and that part of the foundation was actual bedrock—which explains why there isn't a straight wall in the place or a floor that's even remotely level. It was constructed as a single-storied homestead, back in the day, when the surrounding countryside was nothing more than cornfields and dusty roads that quickly turned to mud after heavy spring rains.

As families came and went, additional rooms were added: the kitchen was transformed into a dining room and moved to the back of the house, where the main bathroom eventually ended up in the center adjacent the dining area (which, I can attest, is not the best location after a family dinner of beans). The attic space was converted into two more bedrooms and a half-bath added. Closets were built into rooms that used to accommodate dressers and wardrobes.

The maple flooring throughout the dining room and adjoining kitchen was salvaged from a razed high school gym in Leavenworth, Kansas. I purchased the house from an ex-girlfriend after it had been completely gutted and left vacant for a little over a year—the whole place is still a work in progress.

I love old homes and older neighborhoods—where people understand the value of story wrapped up in the history of a particular time and place. The hand-tooled, carefully crafted screen door; the slightly warped front porch skirted in lattice with skillfully lathed wooden beams supporting a sharply pitched roof; gently worn, painted walls; scuffed and unvarnished hardwood floors; the uneven lines etched in doorframes tracking the height of a growing child—the best of a life that was.

* * *

When I was growing up we weren't allowed to live in this neighborhood, even though I started kindergarten at the grade school just across the street from where I now reside—that was after the decision was issued in Brown vs. the Board of Education. My older siblings all attended the segregated Lincoln School, a dark brick, three-storied edifice located at the corner of Walnut and Poplar on several acres of rough grounds. It was built in the early 1900s to service the educational needs of the town's growing Negro population and covered grades kindergarten through twelve.

My memories of the school are vague, given the fact that I never attended a single class there, but I do remember some of the holiday events that took place throughout most of my grade school years. During summer break the school district would open it up to be used as a playground for our neighborhood, and white teachers who taught in the now, desegregated public schools, would come and teach arts and crafts as a means of keeping our months off less idle. At the end of the season they would bring in a truckload of ice-cold watermelons, and we would eat ourselves sick.

For a short time the building was leased to an obscure toy company that produced an even more obscured toy called a Spin Spin. After the company's failure, it was left unused, and in the late '60s it became the central location for several morning "breakfast" programs put on by the Kansas City Panther Party in their forays outside the urban core into the surrounding suburbs where large pockets of black folks waited out the times.

During one unseasonably hot summer when I was a senior in high school, a cousin of mine was shot by a local man on the street between the old school and the Pentecostal church on the corner. From that moment on its memory was never the same in the neighborhood.

By the late '70s the old school was a dark and ominous reminder of the city's segregated past; having fallen into total disuse, it suffered the fate of all abandoned buildings. Overgrown with thistle and littered with debris and rotted branches from the dead oaks that spotted the campus grounds, it cut a menacing presence against the neighborhood skyline. And with its windows busted out, and basement doors kicked in, the elements quickly took their toll, and wandering drunks who often took up residence in the dank and murky darkness soon fueled the legend that it was haunted.

It was finally demolished in the mid-'80s with the arrival of Urban Renewal. The land was purchased from the city by the local African Methodist Episcopal Church (the same church in which I had taught Sunday school), and a geometrically designed house of worship erected in its place.

Along with the destruction of the old school came the destruction of our tightly woven neighborhood community. Because of how matters of real estate were handled back in the day, most black folks were forced to live on the north side of town, along with a few families of Mexican and Asian descent—Urban Renewal changed all that. Finally given the opportunity to buy or lease property that had otherwise been unavailable, most jumped at the opportunity to integrate into the larger community.

Nearly all of the houses in our old neighborhood were condemned and razed, and those that weren't were reconstructed to be almost unrecognizable. The places that most of us grew up in were so ramshackle and old (having the life lived out of them by the previous white residents), that by the time our families moved in they were already substandard. The only structures to remain untouched throughout the six-block rectangle that framed our isolated community were the Pentecostal church on the corner and the 2nd Baptist church several blocks up the hill.

Writer Thomas Wolfe once wrote: You can't go home again. And for many people it's metaphorically true. But for a lot of black folks it's a much more literal declaration. For many of us there is no physical home to return to...no memory of place to remind us of some of the most poignant times in our lives.

It's more than just having a whole area wiped away—the whole landscape of a childhood growing up. The idea of a place that one could return to when older to evoke and reflect on a life looking backward is not an option. This, I realize, is just one of the many small discernible things that a history of racism steals from us.

* * *

This bothers me—even as I try not to think about it and give it power—those small slights and losses, which have an understated way of diminishing the quality of one's life on so many minute levels. The fact that many of us never learned to swim because we weren't allowed in public swimming pools, or to purchase quality homes, or own parcels of land that could be passed down as inheritance—small things with huge implications—the subtleties of racism's residue. One is forced to acknowledge the loss of opportunities tied to the tincture of skin.

Ah. "Thou dost protest too much," one might say. But in the real world, race matters and the simplest of everyday things are wrought with its complications.

Reaching back into the memory of childhood, I can recall the many vacation trips my parents would take us on to visit neighboring relatives. They would carefully plot out the route the night before, purposely avoiding those municipalities that posted signs on their outskirts informing us not to get caught in town after sunset. On one such trip, with the gas tank idling near empty, my father sought to fill it up, only to be turned away at every station. I remember my mother crying.

In researching his book, *Sundown Towns: A Hidden Dimension of American Racism*, author James Loewen first thought that he might discover maybe forty such cities strewn about the country—towns that literally forbade blacks and other minorities to be present in them after sunset. To his amazement he ended up categorizing over one thousand, some in the Deep South, but nearly seventy percent in the Northern and Midwestern states, giving credence to the old civil-rights adage: In the south they called it Jim Crow, and in the north they called it Dr. James Crow.

I'm honest enough to admit that this often hidden aspect of American culture, is still just that—and all across this great country of ours, are hundreds of small to medium-sized townships that house few if any people of color at all. And I would be even more dishonest to think that I could trek across the country questioning its populace with the same ease as William Least Heat-Moon in his popular travelogue *Blue Highways*.

Color me cynical not to imagine that the majority of those cities, if not all, were Sundown Towns at some point, with signs posted just outside their city limits. And Least Heat-Moon, despite his indigenous surname (a reference to his Osage ancestry), easily passes for white in his travels.

This is but another of those small inequities that quietly gets overlooked. My grandmother was a full-blooded Kickapoo native, which would have given my father half that lineage, and me, at least a quarter. But the "one drop" rule, instituted by white folks back then, wiped out his entire indigenous genealogy by simply proclaiming him Negro or Colored. It offends me at times to think that some people, who travel through their lives as white, will at some point conveniently declare that quarter-blood for scholastic reparations and such (laying claim to everything but the burden), while I, because of that one purposeful act, have no similar recourse.

Don't misunderstand me. I enjoy Least Heat-Moon's writings, and listening to him talk about both the landscape and people moves me to reminisce about a much simpler time. But I would be deluding myself in thinking I could have a similar experience.

* * *

There is a cruelty in the history of this country that closely borders on evil, and it comes from denying a past replete with unfairness and privilege. It readily forgets about the Jim Crow-ism and lynching, the laws that made it impossible for some to purchase land and property or be given a good paying job, or, how nepotism and "good ole boy" networking were but two of the many gateway to white privilege and class status.

It seldom acknowledges the financing of one's own oppression through taxation that never benefited your schools or neighborhoods; or the purposeful red lining that locked people away in concrete high rises out of sight and mind. It overlooks, and rather conveniently, the homes and towns burned out from anger torched by lies of rape or accidental acts of non-compliance to regulations that declared you less than human.

Nothing is simple or easy as a Black man in America, and everything once again becomes suspect. Still, you're called upon to be better than your past circumstances, to seek the higher ground. It's a strange double standard that I will never be comfortable with.

*                    *                    *

I got up earlier than usual today. Downstairs the house was cool and quiet, the only sound coming from the ticking of an old wall clock that no longer chimes. I splashed water on my face and made coffee and, while it was brewing, stepped out onto the front porch into the early-morning darkness.

The air outside was brisk and clean, and the soft morning breeze played an improvised melody on the wind chimes hanging from the open rafters. I pulled back the living room blinds to let the first light of day weave its way into the room. Settling back for a moment to sip and read, I came across this wonderful Buddhist inspired quip from author Mark Nepo, from his script *Awakening*: "One key to knowing joy is being easily pleased."

I am so easily pleased. That doesn't mean that I don't have high standards or values, only that I'm all right with whatever moment and experience I find myself in. To be sure, this has always been my fall-back default whenever life gets overwhelming and I begin to question the fairness of it all. I take a moment to reflect and remember the blessing.

It's been said that God, foreseeing the hardship that black folks were to endure, blessed them with a youthfulness in both physicality and spirit. I don't know if that's true, but I do know that, for a people who have known the heart of darkness, cursed, shamed and abused, who are often viewed as the pariahs of the world—the essence of joy is an enduring presence.

It's about being at ease in a world that's uneasy with your being present. It's discovery: finding the wealth in poverty, the celebration in service, the forgiveness in hate, and the deliverance in love. It's about being unsatisfied yet easily pleased.

*                    *                    *

The air is moist and cool as it tiptoes through the open living room windows, curling the pages of my open book. And in the background, just above the soft breaking of the morning sun, the late saxophonist Grover Washington Jr. is "moonstreaming" on the stereo.

Holiday mornings are another kind of Sunday, full of laziness and sunshine, especially after rain. On such mornings, even God is tempted to sleep in.

*"This is what one thirsts for, I realize, after the smallness of the day,*
*of work, of details, of intimacy--even of communication,*
*One thirsts for the magnitude and universality of a night full*
*of stars, pouring into one like a fresh tide."*
*-Anne Morrow Lindbergh*

# Summer

*"The summer sun was not meant for boys like me."*
*- Benjamin Alire Sáenz*

# June

## S M T W T F S

Early this morning a brief storm swept through, gently nudging me awake. Inside, the house was warm and stuffy, and when I opened the front room windows the wind came rushing in with a chill that instantly cooled the room and brought Goosebumps to my arms.

Later, as I sat out on the back deck, I looked up at a wash of wispy gray and white clouds painted against a pastel blue sky. The sun was just beginning to rise, and further off to the west, framed by low-hanging branches, the receding clouds unveiled a dark blue horizon.

Once again, I am in awe of this unfolding day.

* * *

As far back as I can remember, I was always an early riser. Waking up an hour or so before sunrise, I would quietly slip out the back door and go for walks along the railroad tracks that separated my neighborhood from the rest of town. There's just something about inhabiting the space of early morning that really hushes the spirit, and to this day, I still get a quiet quickening in doing so.

So, I decided to take off work today. It's seldom planned when I do this, but my job is a solitary one, in some ways a reflection of a lifestyle I've always chosen. For me, being alone has never translated into being lonely, and I crave the freedom of motion, to be able to move about at my own pace regardless of my responsibilities.

I once took a job as a graphic design artist for a mid-size printing company—I lasted a little over a week. I remember being held hostage inside a small cubical surrounded by a gang of talented but frustrated and disgruntled artists, each having succumbed to the passing of time and the dictates of a life they never wanted; tied to a time clock and stuck in a job that had them touching up logos and artwork created by others. It was production employment in its worst form, especially for creative people who yearned to produce and develop ideas of their own. Needless to say, I was not long for that world.

* * *

In the spring of 1978, my youngest brother was killed in an automobile accident. He was twenty-four and I was living in Colorado at the time. I cried all night when I got the news of his death; it hurt my heart so deeply...and I remember the only solace I found that night was in the arms of my cousin's boyfriend. He held me close and let me sob into his chest, and it was the first time I realized that I could be physically consoled by a man and still maintain both my sense of heterosexuality and masculinity.

I loved my brother, who towered above me by nearly five inches. He was lanky tall, quiet and suffered from Tourette's syndrome—a continuous blinking that I think now probably played some part in his accident on that cold, rainy April morning. He had a passion for comic books (something that we all shared and passed down one to the other as we were growing up), and wanted to be an artist for Marvel Comics. Truly ironic when you consider his first name was Stanley (Stan Lee).

I remember seeing my father cry for the first time ever, and for the only time thereafter. Sitting next to my mother at the funeral home with his huge hands shielding his face, he wept silently throughout the service. Not even the death of his remaining brother and sister, who passed years before him, had such a saddening effect as that of my brother—the youngest of his five sons.

The early death of my brother...the shoulder of my cousin's boyfriend...the quiet tears of my father—all profoundly affected my sense of self and helped sketch the profile of the person I am today.

* * *

In a tattered shoebox, stuff with high school memorabilia and odd clippings, there's a clear plastic cassette tape with the word PRIVATE scrawled across the top in faded, but perfectly printed, black letters. Held there, frozen in time on a magnetic strip of cellophane, are the intonation and nuances of the youngest of my brothers, who passed away more than thirty years ago.

I discovered the tape while packing up his room shortly after his death; in an effort to assist my parents who were not up to the job of doing it. And in listening to it back then, I rediscovered the boy I grew up with: his joyful laugh and peculiar sense of humor...his distinctive thoughtful side...the secrets we hide; the mysteries that only we know about ourselves.

I don't know when or why he made the recording. Maybe he had a premonition that he would not be long to this world and wanted someone to know something of the boy who loved art, and dreamed of making comic books through awkward sounds and stammering.

I find thinking about him difficult and writing about him even more so, and as much as I would like to listen to the tape...hear the voice I harmonized with on all those Sunday morning services…I'm hesitant to do so, fearing what sensations it might disclose. And though I can scarcely remember the content of the tape, its essences was a joy I had never forgotten in its revelation of knowing all that I didn't know about him.

This is true of people in general, but especially of those who operate within the perimeter of our lives—that their lives are uniquely their own, and no matter how much we love them…no matter how close they might appear…the reality of their days will always be unknown to us. There will always be experiences we'll never share, lovers we'll never understand, and passions that take us totally by surprise. And to express with certainty, that we know another, is the greatest deception perpetrated against ourselves and them.

But this is a good thing. To never truly know another is to understand and appreciate the infinite unfolding of who they are and all that they might be. To be surprised by what we thought was known and familiar is to embrace mystery… cup it in our hands that we might know the feel of it… press it to our ears that we might hear the sound of it…touch it to our lips that we might taste its bitter sweetness and know its essence as a true reflection of what was but will never be again.

And this, I realize, is what I fear most. To know what was once known, but now forgotten: the song of his voice; the reopening of a wound that has never healed... the reality of a loss that will never be replaced. It happens across the whole wide world every day, a million times over, the sudden loss of life...creating a void in a space once filled with familiarity...the crooked smile, the nappy hair...a laugh and way of walking inherited from those who came before.

We fill that space in the care of those left behind; the image fades but is never truly forgotten. And sometimes...during really quiet moments...or in between the rush of early morning traffic...we think of them...their gentle way...their giving heart...their enduring spirit unaltered by the passing of time or the absence of presence...in the sweet, soft, surrender of solitude we smile...having known their love.

So, for now I have the memory of him: roughhousing on the living room floor, singing on the front porch stoop, creating comic books at the dining room table—poignant vignettes tenderly tucked away in the gray matter of my mind., and for now, that is enough.

*          *          *

Outside the air is cool and thick; heavy with humidity. It's early, about five-thirty, and between the tangle of low-hanging branches I can just make out the penumbra moon glowing crimson/yellow against the pale blue wash of the morning sky.

I love these early-summer mornings just before sunrise; the sky a shadowy presences against the lighted streetscape, and in the distance, the soft, mournful wail of a passing train. I'm reminded that life is lived at the speed of now.

It's so easy to get caught up in the mundane circumstance of living. It's so easy to fall into the rut of getting up, going to work and doing all the etceteras in between: shopping, continuing education, paying the mortgage—watching life instead of engaging it.

I have so much to do today: laundry, mow the lawn, buy new tires for the car. And that's the good stuff. Still, I find respite in the solitude of this moment, as writer Anne Morrow Lindbergh so movingly describes, "...pouring into one like a fresh tide."

*          *          *

When my brother died, an old girlfriend got in touch with me to offer her condolences. She was actually the first real love of my life, back when I was about twenty-one and the summer sizzled hot and humid and fresh with the promise of forever.

I remember the ambivalence I felt at taking the call and hearing her voice. Even though it had been just shy of a year or so since we had last spoke, the breakup had not been very agreeable—which is often the case in relationships between men and women. Looking back, in all honesty, I have to admit that she simply outgrew me, which isn't an easy thing to own up to. But I think women do this a lot more often than men.

I was never one to be cynical about love—probably overly sentimental, if anything. I was a true follower, at one point; in the hippie kind of Finnian's Rainbow kind of love. All love, peace and misunderstanding. It took nearly forty years for the world to finally beat that crap out of me. I know that sounds cynical, but I think it's a little more like being worn-out.

Back in the day, I would fall in love at the drop of my pants, confusing lust with love in the worse tense, possibly because they were both four-letter words. Back then, all that me and my running partners used to talk about was "getting a piece." Our vice was strictly women and sex, which we considered to be one and the same. Even if I liked a girl and wanted to be with her, the inclination to run for the hills after having sex was almost a given. It took the acuity of a maturing mind to understand the difference; that the "piece" was a very precious part of a whole person. Coming to that realization eventually changed the way I experienced women. The sad thing is: It shouldn't have taken so long.

I think she got tired of waiting for me to grow up or, better yet, man up. In nearly every circumstance conceivable, I failed her, and for that I'm sorely ashamed. There are times when I wish I could tell her how sorry I am for not being there; there are times I wish I could talk to her just once more, let her know what a remarkable person she was, and how loving me and being a part of my life at that moment in time influenced the kind of man I still struggle to be.

These days, I think about her often; whenever a sudden summer storm sweeps through and the afternoon is swaddled in humidity and heat…or when the wayward laughter from a young girl passing on the streets catches my ear, and I'm transported back to that moment I first heard her laugh. She had an innocent and gentle way of inhabiting her space on the planet that I didn't quite appreciate and understand, and I feel such a loss for that these days… in this carousel world where people enter and exit our lives like roommates at a college dorm.

**I** used to believe that I had no regrets about the decisions of the past; I used to think that, given the gift to do things over, I would still make the same choices—but now I know, there are some things that we need to be regretful about: not speaking the truth of heart and mind to our siblings and parents…not admitting we were wrong in ending a friendship…not believing in the best that life has to offer…and not loving the person who loved us beyond our faults and failings with an intensity of spirit that might only happen once…literally once in a lifetime.

**I**'m reminded of the haunting words echoed in a poem by writer Mari Evans: If there be sorrow…let it be for things undone/ undreamed/ unrealized/ unattained/ to these add one:/ love withheld/ restrained.

*"I look at you and I would rather look at you than all the portraits in the world."-Frank O'Hara*

* * *

**W**e buried my uncle today. It seems like the last several years have been filled with a mixture of losses; starting with my father, just months before his eighty-eighth birthday; an uncle (my mother's brother) last January; then a cousin (his daughter) several months later. Another uncle (on my father's side) in June, and just this past weekend yet another one of my mother's brothers.

**A**ll of these deaths have given me pause, and today I find myself in a very quiet and reflective place. I've taken off work for the remainder of the week...just wanting to spend some time with myself. I think I'll start by taking a walk in the woods.

*"Because I could not stop for death - He kindly stopped for me."*
*-Emily Dickson*

**T**his morning as I sat on the deck, I leaned back to look up into a gun blue sky, the kind of sky often revealed by a diffusion of light just before the sun rises. And as storm clouds rushed by, their feathery underbelly silhouetted in soft shadows,

I glimpsed a single, shining star and felt the presence of a billion others hidden behind the pale blue morning firmament, and I thought about the millions of years it took that light to travel—for it to be visible to me at that moment…in this time and place…and I understood what a miracle and wonderful opportunity it was to be human and deliciously alive.

*   *   *

Yesterday afternoon I had a young, engaged couple over for dinner and conversation. At first sight you might think them mismatched; he with his dark, unruly long hair and scruffy beard…the kind of beard that only twenty-four year-olds can grow—and she with her long, tangle-free blonde locks framing her small, round face in a soft cascade.

A certified heating and air technician, he dresses with an eclectic style reminiscent of '60s hippies and old '70s counterculture radicals, and is just as prone to wild theory of a conspiratorial nature. She, on the other hand, confesses to a more introspective and introverted sense of self; her response to most questions is metered and slow like that of a teacher responding to inquisitive students—which indeed she is.

However, regardless of these dissimilarities, there is a matched resonance to their coupling that was clearly noticeable. Whenever he spoke, she would listen to him with a soft, dreamy look in her eyes, and a smile ever so slightly would touch the form of her lips. It was as if she were quietly whispering to him, "I really like and admire you—even though you can be a little 'out there' at times."

And at her side, he seemed to acquire a shy sort of puppy-dog demeanor—a subtle yielding of his youthful masculinity to her much gentler and reasonable point of view. Casting quick glances at her between huge bites of barbecue, he paused at one point to tell her she had a small smidgen of sauce beneath her mouth—and the way he said it was evidence of his deep, engaging affection for her.

They were perfect in their dance together.

Maybe this is just the stuff of young love…too new and innocent to be jaded by the circumstance of knowing too much. In their attentive display was a love that I found myself longing for—the understanding and acceptance of another—built upon a foundation of stark differences and shared commonalities. Thinking about them afterward made me hopeful for the future of any romance I might engender.

*"I once had a girl, or should I say, she once had me."*
*-Lennon & McCartney (Norwegian Wood)*

*                    *                    *

Loving someone...anyone...is never a wasted effort. And breaking up with them, regardless of the circumstance, doesn't make them a bad person; just not the right person for us. I don't understand why this is such a hard thing to wrap our brains around. I don't understand jealousy and envy from a current partner or girlfriend, over past relationships.

Maybe that's why I'm still single?

How is it that two people can meet, fall madly in love, have children, raise a family and then some years later divorce and end up hating each other? I mean, this was the person whom at one point you confessed undying love for...who saw you at your worst: head over the toilet with vomit dripping from your nose, or all stuffed up and snotty with a cold or fever.

There was a time when you shared subtle looks, inside jokes, and the same taste in wine and music. All of that suddenly lost to time and familiarity. They say familiarity often breeds contempt because it exposes our flaws—much like newfound lovers caught up in the throes of passion who revel in the freshness of each other—but as time passes and the unknowing becomes known, deficits gradually appear: the crooked smile that charmed us in the beginning becomes a sneer; the cute way she rolls her eyes is suddenly dismissive. Moonlight cascading through an open window falls delicately across the naked form of our lover and shamelessly reveals his bloated pot belly or her cellulite thighs. The innocence that once comforted us is suddenly jaded as we are jolted back to the truth of being human and imperfect.

But being human is all about embracing flaws; our own as well as those of others. And it's so easy for us to forget that it can take one, possibly two lifetimes plus forever to completely understand the complexity of another person, and that enjoying the discovery is half the fun...and to know that loving someone... anyone is seldom an exercise in futility.

That's what my young lovers reminded me of this past Sunday afternoon.

*                    *                    *

I'm nothing like the woman I've been dating. She petite and reticent with a slightly sad disposition; well-educated and bright, introverted and shy in ways that are both challenging and endearing.

On the other hand, I tower just an inch under six feet and have a fairly muscular build. Neither introverted nor extroverted, I was never a good student and don't have a college degree. I am well-read, though, and possess a number of abilities and talents—and a personality that tends to lean toward the up side.

She's White and likes to bake, loves metal and hard rock music, and has a master's in social work and psychology. I eat three squares a day, chill out to jazz, and as a Black man tied to a particular history, boast no real interest in having a Master.

You would think our relationship improbable with its myriad dissimilar points of view and history, but our individual preferences are an acquired choice built upon personal elements that define who we are or choose to be. This is the individual stuff of our character and goes far beyond the superficial aspects of physical appearances or an "alike" mindedness—attributes forged from the fire and metal of our diverse experiences.

We are nothing alike, but have many things in common: a love of books and public TV and radio; good beer and wines; independent movies, home-cooked meals; stormy fall weather; and incredibly uninhibited sex. In the end, it's simply our commonalities (not our likenesses) that draw us together.

It's not unusual for people to seek out persons who share a general resemblance in skin color, eye shape, hair texture and language; and because of that, we tend to believe that we are somehow different from others of our genus. And it's not enough that they look like us; they must imitate us in almost every manner conceivable. So in dating and relationships we search out those who are again most like us in the things they do and say, the way they think and believe, and what they like and dislike: Country music as opposed to rap, rock and roll in opposition to rhythm and blues; Republican/Democrat, secular/divine. We place a whole lot of emphasis on them liking what we consider to be the right things.

But our likes and dislikes are such fickle things—an acquired taste. Given time, most of our preferences change, and open exposure to anything, whether it's a person or object, can have a dramatic effect on how we think and feel and the conclusions we draw.

Being alike isn't always a comparable substitute for compatibility. We tend to think of bigotry in terms of race, but in its clearest description, it usually pertains to an attitude of narrow mindedness in both thoughts and deeds, and particularly, in regards to opinions that differ from those of our own. One way of overcoming both our personal and public bias is deference for our commonalities.

What we have in common are usually the finer attributes of our character: a respect for honesty, fairness and understanding; having a sense of humor and empathy, compassion, and a sensitivity that is both considerate and moral. These defining traits are the bedrock on which any relationship can be solidly built.

If I can respect you as a person, see you as unique in reference to my own distinctiveness, then liking the things that you like is simply an added bonus.

*"The encounter is a meeting of harmony and mutuality, a feeling of being within the life of another person while at the same time maintaining one's own identity and individuality."*
*—Clark E. Moustakas*

* * *

I don't believe in *"soul mates,"* at least not in the way that I used to and is still so popular today. I do believe that it's possible to meet someone and in that instant know that there's a connection of some sort. It doesn't happen very often. But it does happen.

We tend to believe that love is an unruly emotion—some fairytale spell we fall under in the wink of a moment, or something that can't be turned off and on like a bathtub faucet. But I think that's true of any feelings that come with emotional involvement. And love is simply that, an emotion, albeit a strong one. Then again, so too are anger, hate and sorrow. We are not slaves to our emotions; if we were, then all acts of passion could be justified.

Our first love is probably our truest love, but that doesn't necessarily make it our true love. The universe, I'm finding out these days, is way too immense for that. We limit love the same way we limit our capacity to express it—by holding it to ridiculous standards and propping it up with our presumptions and prejudices. We love more from a position of lack than we do from a place of personal security, or from a place of knowing who we really are when we're alone and find the world against us.

We want a love built on sacrifice, one that proves it's worthy of us being there, because in the end, we want a love that's guaranteed to last forever. However, few things last forever, especially in the realm of the human heart, and to ask for an undying love is to ask for the heart to never grow beyond its present understanding. It is to ask for the individual to never change with regard to feeling whole and complete.

I'm not defending infidelity or the casualness to commitment that's so prevalent in today's relationships, but loving someone is easy. Liking them for who they are as a vibrant and autonomous human being is a whole other thing. It's possible to love someone and not like who they are. We do this all the time with our siblings and relatives and most intimate partners.

We're seldom who we really are at the start of any relationship, not because we are dishonest, but because it's one of the rare times when we actually are our own best. That's the real paradox. And if all the inner work has been done, we'll find ourselves uniquely present in the potential to be who we fully are—to ourselves and to another—and that will make all the difference in the kind of relationship we'll have.

But the inner work is seldom done—that's the sad part. We come into the coupling even less than half the whole required at making it real and lasting. We do it because it's what our parents wanted, or because our biological clock is ticking. We forge our feelings, fake our orgasms and hide our insecurities. In the end, when it fails, we go about blaming everything but our incomplete selves.

I refuse to get caught up in that.

*　　　*　　　*

I used to take a lot of flak for dating White girls. And some people (both Black and White) often saw my strong sense of Afrocentricity as a contradiction in doing so. But an Afrocentric sensibility is a mainstay for any Black person wishing to navigate the treacherous landscape of the North American continent. It's a worldview that is not only right, but necessary in understanding that who I am as a person of African descent, and the way I think and behave on a cellular level, isn't that far-removed from those of my ancestors on the Motherland.

Still, there was a time when I did question these affairs. I wasn't sure if they were subconscious inclinations based upon my weak sense of self, or simply happenstance. Slavery and assimilation are such subtle diseases of the psyche, especially for Black folks whose sense of worth was so strongly chained to the dominant society for more than four hundred years.

Slavery sickened us as a people on so many levels. And how could it not? When your very humanity is stripped away and made shameful, people tend to do an awful lot of harmful things to themselves and others like them, just to make up for the loss in spirit.

And at its worse, assimilation will have you denying everything that's real about yourself. It will drive you to straighten your hair and lighten your skin with chemicals and bleaches that are toxic to both your mind and body. It'll have you cutting off your nose and biting your lips in order to make them appear thinner—hating the dark, natural patina of your skin; the round curvaceous protrusion of your backside; the soft and supple thickness of your thighs. All the while, a "*different other*" artificially tans, and takes surgeries and injections to fatten their lips and buttocks in feeble attempts to imitate the same naturalness they so fervently malign.

An Afrocentric perspective allows you to understand and respect yourself beyond the comparisons to others. It was important for me to come to this understanding. When a person is secure in the knowledge of himself and where he comes from, when he figures out that some things are both cultural and intrinsic to his identity, he'll no longer feel the need to judge other people and things by external standards that are not his own.

Accepting myself makes it possible for me to accept you regardless of our physical differences. You are no more or less, better or worse, just unalike and wonderfully human. And that's what I discovered in dating: that my preference in the end was simply...women, regardless of their ethnicity, or, age. That circumstance, availability, and the openness of each individual played a key role in any relationship that was to develop.

Do I love Black women? Of course I love Black women. My mother was a Black woman and, so were my sisters and aunts and cousins and just about all my boyhood lovers. I grew up in a neighborhood surrounded by Black women both young and old, and my relationship to them is intimately etched into the stone-matter of my DNA; in subtle ways that I am only now beginning to appreciate.

I am made proud by the sassiness of their spirit, the wit of their mentality and the underrated wisdom of their discerning. I am enthralled by the diversity of their colors, captivated by the beauty of their being exhibited in the full pout of their lips…the broad sweep of their nose… the pliant curve of their backside, the thick of their hips, the girth of their thighs, the natural texture of their hair, nappy and unadorned. Their eyes shine with the joy and the suffering of a femininity that has stood the test of time.

Yes. I love Black women. And I am unequivocally Black. Regardless of whom I choose to be in love with, it will always be so.

* * *

This is what I know about myself at this place in my life. I am not your everyman —never have been…never will be. That's probably why I never married, or had children, which is a great loss because I would've been an exceptional dad and an extraordinary husband (at least I'd like to think so). But in spite of those two missed opportunities, I'm the best I've ever been, and pretty much all right with who I am.

I have loved and lost enough to understand that real love is not the selling of my soul to another, but rather a giving of my heart—honestly, freely—with the essence of who I am firmly tethered to an audacious sense of self.

I am not afraid to love. I am not afraid to give my heart, to be rejected, to cry my eyes out; heal my wounded spirit and begin again…to remain forever open to the act of loving. And here's the kicker: I deserve a real love. A strong love. A sustaining love. A love grounded in the belief that things can and will be better. I don't need a similar personality, ethnicity or mind-set or political persuasion. I'm a woman's man, who, if anything, needs a woman who is her own, who respects the inimitable essences of her nature and brings that fully to the table.

Growing older is a Pinocchio experience; you learn that you don't have to lie to yourself or anyone else anymore about who you are or want to be.

I need a "real live girl" to go with my "real live boy" attitude. No Geppetto could ask for more.

*"There is a mystical organization for singles, "Sex Without Partners," that has a membership composed of many who suffer from unrequited love. Application is free and you can participate without leaving home."*
*-Gordon Livingston, MD*

# August

## S M T W T F S

Outside the sun is shining bright; all the windows in the house are open wide; and the gentle morning breeze is streaming a cool current of air through the downstairs living room and on out the back screen door onto the deck where I sit reading. I'm sipping hot coffee with a French twist and a touch of dark liqueur, while above me the clouds shift in playful patterns against the pastel, blue august sky.

Here, in this moment, I'm reminded of a wonderful quote by Gregg Levoy, from his remarkable tome *Callings*: "There is life in its flesh and toothsome grandeur... all the spill and stomp and shout of it...all the come and go of it...all of it on the one hand waiting for us to act...and on the other rushing down the hourglass."

* * *

From the moment we enter this world we are in a continuous stream of loss. We lose the comfort of the womb to being born, we lose our virginity and innocence to experience, and our youth to time. We lose our hair, our looks, our virility, the people we love—and some of us even lose our minds. We step upon the planet unprepared for all the losses we will encounter at every stage and age of our life, and to that end, we come to know that living is a temporal state.

From the second we're born we begin dying; that birth is a miracle seldom appreciated, and aging a mystery that science has failed to understand, because the body, despite its ability to renew its cells in a thousand myriad ways, still withers and dies in the end.

But there were so many other losses unrelated to death: the loss of my job of eight years for reasons that were highly suspicious; the loss of a ten-year-old friendship that started when two people decided they liked each other, then made a concerted effort to nurture a relationship; and last, but never least, the loss of faith that things on a world level would ever get any better.

Of all those losses, I find the last most troubling. Death we expect; it's the final exit in a finite life. Its specter looms incessantly, waiting for that sudden calamity as we casually go about our day. Losing anyone to the circumstance of living is always a sad thing.

And jobs come and go, especially in these times of automated technologies and narcissistic capitalism; where advancement and opportunity are seldom linked to hard work and merit, but rather to bottom-line agendas that both steal and rob the spirit of the individual worker. Few things in this world are as disappointing as not being paid what you're worth, or, being terminated for reasons you'll never know or are flimsy at best.

In today's world the motto and mission statement for the business community can easily be summed up in the words of *Wall Street*'s Gordon Grecko: "Greed is good."

*"Unbridled capitalism is a highway to nowhere."—Jeremy Irons*

Friendships are another thing that come and go; and as heartbreaking as that may seem, authentic living has a way of whittling out those who can't make the cut. People should bring out the best in us, especially in our most private and intimate relationships, because it's only through our relationships with others that who we are is fully revealed. But that's seldom the case. So the responsibility to bring out the best in us is ours alone, regardless of other people's actions. The best friendships come from giving and sharing; from voicing opinions and experiences that have a way of both informing and enlightening us. They're not about trying to change us, because who we are, or want to be, is too precious an aspiration to be left to the dictates of others.

* * *

I have left a lot of people in my life, and a lot of people have left me. I don't know if I've always made the best decision concerning that act, but I do know that something about them or the situation changed; became disturbing enough that I eventually had to distance myself from the relationship. Usually it had something to do with a particular act or the character of the individual. They turned out not to be the person I first thought they were, or started doing things that I found a little reprehensible. I'm sure those who left me felt the same. How I disappointed them in a thousand different ways.

It's hard leaving people behind. They weave themselves into the fabric of our life and become a part of the garment we wrap around ourselves. Through shared secrets and growing children, job losses and dying parents, the glorious ups and the bone-crushing downs; the many circumstances of life that break our heart or bring us joy. Their exit, whether by accident or choice, leaves an indelible mark upon the canvas of our life, in the sweeping context of the portrait we paint of ourselves.

In most cases, at least for me, those relationships ended because what some people demanded was not congruent with who I was or wanted to be. In his book *Finding Yourself, Finding Other*, psychologist Clarke Moustakas asserts: "When the persons in our world do not offer identifications that permit genuine commitment and engagements, then we must reach beyond these persons. We must learn to live with the uncertainty of creating a new world and endure the tensions of doubt and fear as we struggle to create a beginning that honors our own individuality and selfhood."

Honoring our own individuality and selfhood is a mainstay of identity; that being said, we usually end up with one or two really close confidants. And to have even one such person is a great blessing.

And like friendships, lovers, too, go their own way, and hopefully the parting will be amicable. It's quite possible to conclude that some things aren't meant to last forever. It's quite possible to surmise that some people show up in our lives to teach us something more about who we are, regardless of how painful it might be.

Sometimes loving someone might come down to admitting that they may not be good for us in the long run, or vice versa; that the spark which ignited a relationship was just that, a spark, and never reached the heat of becoming a flame, so it eventually extinguished itself.

Maybe because the children had all grown, maybe because we took too much for granted; maybe because we had not fully come unto our own, and that first twinge of excitement, that desire of wanting to be known by someone other than those who knew us when, was both intoxicating and new.

Whatever the reason, the love we thought would sustain us, burdens us instead, and we are called upon to make the harsh decision. And the truth of the matter is simple, breaking up with someone doesn't make them a bad person…just not the right person for us, because sometimes even loving somebody is not enough.

* * *

But to lose faith in the belief that life is good and will continue to get better is the first crack in the conviction that the "Universe is a friendly place," a quote attributed to Albert Einstein in response to what he believed to be the most critical question one could ask concerning their personal belief. And here, lately, I've begun to find myself feeling unsure about a lot of things—mostly about God and the world around me. At first I thought I might be having a "crisis of faith," but now I know that it's something much more subtle than that.

It's not that I doubt God's existence—no, there's no way, when I look at the miracle of just being alive and a complicated human being, that I could ever doubt the involvement of a creative, benevolent Spirit. I just don't feel as secure as I used to feel about understanding just what it is She/He is doing…or just how much She/He participates in my day-to-day life.

There was a time I used to pray for strength and understanding, never so much for things, but, rather, attributes that would make me more. Better. I always felt that being supported in that way made it possible for me to accomplish any undertaking concerning the acquisition of things. People and the circumstance of living have always mattered so much more to me…and still do to this day.

But at this stage of living, I'm beginning to understand that the meek may "inherit the earth," but seem to lose out on the present moment, and when it comes right down to it, the present moment is really all there is.

Don't get me wrong. I still believe that there will be a reckoning, an ending, but somehow things just don't seem to fit the way that I learned in Sunday school. I guess in the end it all comes down to faith.

Just to be human is to be full of doubt. We're such fragmented and misaligned creatures; slaves to all our secular characteristics and habits. We're constantly seeking the spiritual, the enlightenment, but it always seems to hover just outside our reach, and so we find ourselves constantly grasping at dreams that seldom make it through the night.

I've always enjoyed being human, flawed and imperfect. But maybe that's not the way of Spirit? The fall from grace was all about becoming imperfect, flawed. And the return to grace is all about recapturing a state of perfection. There seems to be so much contradiction in understanding and accepting scripture or, rather, our interpretation of it.

Sometimes I wonder if Spirit foresaw that the struggles in life would be the catalyst for so much of its virtue; that overcoming the trials and tribulations of an imperfect world would lead us to our most rewarding experiences. The desire to fight, to challenge what ails and afflicts us, seems so ingrained.

Sometimes it's the only thing that gives purpose to our life. Sometimes, only in overcoming conflict do we find respite.

*　　　　　*　　　　　*

So now I know that it wasn't so much a "crisis of faith," but rather a moment of deep reflection steeped in the current situation of my existence. I was beginning to wonder: *Where was the serendipity that once influenced my life... the synchronicity...the small God moments that let me know I was being watched over by something more than the twin fates of chance and circumstance?*

Nearly thirty years ago, in another life, I had a heart attack. The trauma of that moment changed that life forever and sent me hurtling across vast constellations of self-discovery, and through it all I have always felt safe. That's what's so currently disconcerting—the ambivalence, the uncertainty, the loss of perspective that faith has always given me.

There aren't many universal truths, and almost all of them involve the natural world. The sun rises in the east and sets in the west, the earth revolves around the sun, and the changing of the seasons is a cleansing of our destructive ways. All other truths are simply conceptual: religion, time, the constitution, and the way we perceive another's heart.

Then there are individual truths that only pertain to the person—they are simply our preferences built upon the foundation of our own experiences and conclusions. That's why what is a truth for you may not be a truth for me, because our circumstances will be different and in essence will change the course of our reasoning.

A belief in God or some sustaining, benevolent Spirit is such a personal and self-defining thing. I come to this belief naturally, and through a consideration that is both cultural and historic. The fact that I come from a people of faith, and a history of folks who despite all odds survived because of their spiritual conviction and understanding, is very edifying.

For them, as well as for me, this Spirit is dichotomous—both real and abstract—and seldom bound by western, linear thinking. Its existence isn't a matter of religious dogma; rather, a visceral appreciation of the intangible rooted in the faithfulness of the tangible. It's an active Spirit capable of not only hearing my prayers but responding to them in small, discernible ways that fall just short of being miracles, and not the proclamations of some pasty, white-bearded, indifferent, rule-making authoritarian lacking any sense of empathy.

It's been said that the "fall from grace" first happened when Adam and Eve were expelled from the Garden, and since then, the further away we get from that original falling the more horrific things become and the worse we seem to treat each other. From the looks of things, it appears we just keep falling and falling farther and farther away; forever failing to give ourselves any chance at redemption.

*"Beyond a certain point, faith is the magic lamp*
*and humility is the abracadabra."*
*-Gregg Levoy*

*"And I rose..In rainy autumn..And walked abroad in a shower of all my days." — Dylan Thomas*

# September

S M T W T F S

On this first day of September, with autumn hiding just around the corner, the forecast calls for temperatures to be in the low hundreds—which is not that unusual for this particular time of the year. They call this period of dry heat and sun the "dog days" of summer (from the Latin: dies caniculares), and in reference to Sirius, the "Dog Star" whose brightness in the heavens at this time of year is only rivaled by the sun.

As a young boy growing up in rural Kansas, these hot, dry days echoed the end of summer and the start of a new school year. On such days I would rise early and walk the railroad tracks on the outskirts of town—before the air turned hot, thick and heavy with the heat of the day.

I loved those "dog days." They were lazy stretches of time, and moments that ushered in the ending as well as the beginning of so many things. That doesn't seem to happen much anymore.

*　　　　*　　　　*

Yesterday, I spent the better part of the morning and afternoon with a good friend. She'd moved recently from a huge house way out in the country to a much smaller cottage in the suburbs. Visiting with her is always a wonderful experience.

A small, springy woman, with bright, round, brown eyes and short, cropped brown hair heavily laced with strands of grey—she has a way of inhabiting her life that I have often tried to emulate. A coinsurer of the unique when it comes to bread, cheese and wine, a simple brunch becomes an inimitable experience, even though it happens again and again, it's always different, new and exciting. And yesterday was no exception.

After a brief tour of the house, we settled in the kitchen, where she quietly began to assemble a "ham sandwich" with her usual English twist. Some fresh, firm, grainy bread she had stumbled across while out shopping—sliced from an elongate loaf and then halved. She gently toasted it, smearing one half with a generous swipe of mayo, and the other with an equal dollop of a spicy jalapeño spread. Several thin folds of mildly flavored ham with sliced romas and red leaf lettuce.

But the real kicker was the cheese. Instead of Swiss or provolone, with its smooth, soft texture, she chose a hard and pungent curd so dry it nearly disintegrated upon slicing. Nestled in crumbly slivers between the ham and sliced tomatoes, I expected such a pairing of so many contrasting ingredients to assault my taste buds, but it teased them instead—the bitter bite of the cheese and mild spiciness of the mashed peppers complimenting each other in a tangy cascade of flavors. She rounded out the small feast with a goblet of stout, chilled lemonade, with slices of avocado and small chunks of a hybrid honeydew melon..

We share a delight for the classics, which is probably the reason our relationship has lasted nearly two decades now. Just several years shy of being five years older than me; we met fourteen-odd years ago when I was in my forties and on the rebound from a failed engagement. She was in her early fifties, her husband having died several years earlier.

Back then, she was an exquisite, shapely and petite middle-aged woman with well-toned arms, and a round firm derriere that yielded easily to the touch. For a short time we were lovers, but came to be better friends. We use to go for long hikes in the woods just outside of town, where she would amaze me with her impeccable knowledge of wildflowers and birds.

These days she is more than less the shadow of that former self. One blotched hip replacement later and recently retired—her gait has slowed to a carefully etched walk, her activities tempered with exhaustion. Though still a handsome woman, she seems smaller, more fragile. Growing older has a way of ambushing us. It's such a subtle thing, this lessening of physical ability and memory.

*　　　　*　　　　*

I seem to be aging far better than most of my contemporaries and peers—which can be a little disconcerting. I was totally oblivious to this until one day (over thirty-five years ago), a close friend pointed it out.

We were standing in front of a huge picture window at her home when she softly whispered in my ear, "You know, you're not aging like the rest of us," then left to retrieve the afternoon mail. I watched her from inside the house, and in that moment it dawned on me: She had grown older. It was clearly evident in the way she walked, stooped and kneeled.

That particular revelation continues to haunts me. On a good day I can easily pass for someone in his late thirties; on a bad day, forty-five. Either day has me looking at least fifteen to twenty years younger than I actually am. Couple that with our natural inclination to not feel as old inside as we look outside, and you have a formula for a myriad of misunderstandings.

I tend to date women fifteen to twenty years my junior, and on occasion have flirted openly with those even younger. This isn't a preference but simply my inclination (no matter how misguided) to inadvertently not take my age into consideration. And having a youthful appearance is not a necessary reminder. I've often joked that somewhere sheltered away in some closet attic, a portrait hangs, shouldering the days, growing older with each passing season.

It's a peculiar curse—this aging gracefully.

*"It is a privilege to age...it is a privilege to grow old." –Laura Linney*

*　　　　*　　　　*

I like growing older. There's something liberating about it. Growing up is such a Charlie Brown, "wishy-washy" experience—suffering the angst of always wanting to be grown-up or something other than what we are at the time—but growing older has a way of freeing us from all our fears and failings. There's nothing to prove to ourselves or anyone else anymore, so very little time is wasted on things and people that don't engage us or move us forward into greater and more real experiences.

There was a time when I thought nothing could be better than youthfulness, and I viewed aging as a curse, something to be dreaded, especially its physical aspects: wrinkling skin and hair loss, the lessening of sight and sound. And it's true that these are difficult things to come to terms with, but they're merely a natural part of our coming full circle in a finite life.

Having lived now for more than a half-century, I know that time can often be extended beyond the norm. Attitude, nutrition and a sense of spirituality are just some of the things that make this possible, and once embraced with an open heart and an honest awareness, their capacity to move us further along the time line of our earthly existence allows us to tap into the blessings of the "fountain of youth" that is our spirit.

So, the true curse of growing older lies not so much in our physical lessening, as in our unwillingness to change, and not only with the times, but away from the clichés and lifestyles we cling to so tenaciously. Antiquated ways of thinking and believing passed down to us like treasured heirlooms, but never really appraised of their current value—if there were ever sins of the parents inherited by the children, it has to be in the narrow-minded legacy of opinionated rationalizations we pass on as definitive truths.

Growing older frees us of those false truths and offers us both its blessings and its curses. But its blessings are more apparent in all the ways we come to know ourselves, our truths, our values—and even better than knowing who we are, is the satisfaction derived from liking who we have become. Nothing...nothing is more liberating than that.

* * *

The one problem I find with growing older is that most people believe they need to have enough money to maintain their current lifestyle. But our lifestyle at thirty is not the same as the one we need at sixty. Let's be honest. After a certain point in life, we're basically on our way out. Acquiring a bigger house and newer car are simply not that important or necessary anymore. The kids are grown and usually have families of their own, and that four-bedroom dream house that once reverberated with laughter and the patter of little feet is now quiet, haunted by the memories of times gone by.

It's hard, I know, to give up the things we knew, but life demands it, and growing older, like a flame, burns away the best of times. Still, this life at sixty is truly some kind of wonderful.

* * *

This morning, after a gallant effort by the sun to shine, a storm moved in. Gently bullying the sun back behind dark clouds of rain and lightning, it came on strong and fast, stomping thunder, huffing and puffing and threatening to blow the house down.

Instead, it took out the huge elm that towered nearly four stories above my house in the yard across the alley that separates me from my closest neighbor.

At first I thought it was just the crackling of lightning as it came crashing to the ground, shaking the house and barely missing my car by inches; its crooked and broken branches like massive, arthritic fingers stretching out across the front lawn.

As the rain continued to fall in slanted sheets, the wind whipped fitfully at the remaining branch, even taller than the one it had just taken, and threaten to rip it also. Then as quickly as it had begun, it suddenly relented, quietly moving on like some elemental David, satisfied with having humbled the Goliath elm.

I am always amazed at the power of Mother Nature and the fury of her vengeance. We have scorned her too deeply, too callously in these last several decades as to expect anything other from her. Like most things feminine, she forgives easily, but has her limit…her tipping point. In her spurring, both men and trees are left rent and broken. In acknowledging the power of her love, we are healed.

*"How strange that Nature does not knock, and yet does not intrude!"*
*-Emily Dickinson*

* * *

Albert Einstein was once asked which question, among all his inquiries into the mysteries of the universe, was the most important question to ask. His response: "Is the universe a friendly place or not?"

I get that, and I do believe that the universe is a friendly place. Not to believe so is to set myself up for a whole bunch of disappointment and doubts. It's sort of like that famous Henry Ford quote of whether you think you can or you think you can't—either way you'll be right.

I also believe that people are basically good. Again, not to believe so is to fall into the habit of being suspect of even the most innocent act. Maybe I'm naïve, but I've always expected and believe in the best of everything, especially the intentions of others. I think I would rather do so, and be proven wrong every once and a while, than to think otherwise. It's not like I'm not paying attention or know that the opposite can be true; it's just that in most difficult circumstances, events and people have always risen to the occasion. Knowing this is a very reassuring thing.

* * *

A big part of believing in a "friendly universe" is the part we personally play in making it so, and there's a lot we can do to stay that course: eat right, exercise, not place ourselves in unreasonable situations. And then there is that small matter of faith which scripture aptly describes as "the substance of things hoped for—evidence of thing not seen." I find that to be such a wonderful and intriguing play on words.

For me, faith is an unexplainable "knowing" that I have about the outcome of things. This is more than positive thinking or pie-in the-sky believing—and almost impossible to explain...but it's a certainty that's easily taken for granted simply because its occurrence is such a background operating mechanism. For me, knowing is the biggest part of doing.

* * *

Lately I've been feeling a little disillusioned, not only with our national state of affairs (where as a country we seem unable to come together for our own collective good), but also with the way we personally handle affairs related to matters of the heart. And I don't mean this strictly in a romantic sense, but in regards to all our relationships— whether societal, communal or familial.

It starts on the most basic of levels: in how we treat that life which we have been given stewardship over; in how we attend not only to the care of the dogs and cats and other domestic animals that share our lives, but also the various creature that provides us sustenance. Failing to treat that life humanely, we easily move on in our disregard for the humanity of those who are like us, but differ in age, race, gender and orientation.

These days, it seems, we can justify anything. Having fallen out of our hearts and into our heads, we rationalize ourselves into believing whatever we want about one another. Moreover, since we have such a low regard for those who are different from us, we often cater to our worse inclinations, such as settling into mean-spirited discourse and snarky exchanges meant to damage and maim.

We like to think of ourselves as a nation that appreciates diversity, but if we're honest, we'd have to admit to being the furthest thing from it. As Americans, we seem to take great pride in our knee-jerk response to the subtleties of other people's realities—especially those who are different from us.

We live in a world of abuser and victim, both suffering from a familiar sickness: a lack of self-esteem. What I've noticed is that if a person isn't comfortable with who they are, they have a propensity to be a lot of undesirable things: homophobic, racist, sexist, and unable to communicate across diverse lines. And what they fail to understand is that when you casually disregard others, you eventually come to disregard even those you love, and in the end everyone suffers.

I don't know if there's really any way to save people who are bigoted (since understanding that type of rationalization eludes me). I don't know if any amount of diversity training will make it possible for some people to actually empathize with those who are less fortunate or are different from them in class and appearance. I do know that people can and do change, but only if they feel the need to or have the inclination. Knowing that, however, sustains me, especially in these times when I'm feeling just a little disillusioned.

*"When life is heaviest with pain and anguish— that is the time when we will dance and sing together to awaken the sleeping God of our own lost hope."—Sheldon Ko*

# OCTOBER

## S M T W T F S

The squirrels have taken to building a nest in the large maple just to the right of the front porch, on the south side of the house. So every morning this week, I've awakened to a sidewalk and yard littered with small twigs and dry branches—the lumber they use to erect their huge, leafy abode in the uppermost reaches of the tree.

I have to admit, for squirrels, they don't seem very deft at this, as I scrape up compost twice the size of what they have attempted to "squirrel" together, so to speak. And for all their assiduous intent, when the maple leaves turn gold and yellow, the late-fall winds strip the tree bare, exposing their domicile to the elements where the constant barrage from the onslaught of winter winds batters it to smithereens.

I watch them go through this year after year, and even though I consider myself the philosophical type, I'm hard-pressed to discern any kind of enlightenment from their labor other than the fact that practice doesn't necessarily make perfect, and instinctual habits aren't necessarily the best way to respond to circumstances of life. On second thought, I think understanding that is enough.

*   *   *

*"It was the best of times, it was the worst of times...we had everything before us, we had nothing before us."*
*-Charles Dickens*

When I was around eighteen, just several summers before Urban Renewal came to town and changed our neighborhood forever, I moved out of my attic bedroom and spent that entire season on the screened-in porch located at the front northeast corner of our house. The summer heat in my attic bedroom had become increasingly unbearable, and so my parents, fully understanding the conditions, allowed me the respite of camping out on the porch that my father had screened in the year before.

That would turn out to be one of the most defining summers of all my boyhood experiences. That summer, I would meet a girl, lose my virginity, get lost in drugs and abandon writing for the next thirteen years. Looking back, I can only say that Dickens was right—"it was the best of times, and the worst of times" all rolled into one.

It was the best of times because it would be the last summer of my innocence. It was the worst of times, because it would be the last summer of my innocence.

I remember reading the *Autobiography of Malcolm X*, and suddenly growing more aware of my separateness from the dominant culture. About that same time, the Kansas City Panther Party started making excursions out of the urban core and into the segregated suburban neighborhoods where many of us lived, setting up workshops and their signature morning pancake breakfasts.

It's been said that, before Malcolm, we were Negroes with emphasis on the capital "N." It was a time when being American was all about assimilation—especially if you were something other than of White, European ancestry. For Black people this was a huge head trip, and invited a whole host of distortions that set up shop in our psychological makeup.

Attempts at bleaching the skin, shortening the nose and pruning the lips; conking the hair straight with acids and dyes; and trying not to appear like anything African were all seen as progressive ways of fitting in. Succumbing to such things was a huge wound to the spirit.

The Brother Minister changed all that.

It was a heady time, and my oldest brother was attending college at Kansas University under an academic scholarship. He lived for a short time at the International House with a host of students from other parts of the world, and was part of the Black Student Union, whose confrontations with campus authorities were widely publicized. I remember how worried my mother became after he started receiving hate mail in response to his letters that were frequently printed in our local newspaper.

I was just twelve years old when Malcolm X was gunned down in '64 at the Audubon Ballroom in Harlem, and sixteen when King was assassinated just four years later on the balcony of the Lorraine Hotel in Memphis. These are faded memories, filled at the time with both fear and anger, as well as a gnawing uncertainty about the future and what it held.

It was during that long, hot summer that I stopped doing comic book art and started doing Black Art. Family Circle and Good Housekeeping were replaced by subscriptions of Ebony, Jet and Essence magazines. And the huge jar of Vaseline petroleum jelly that dominated the vanity counter was swapped out with Afro Sheen and Stay-Soft-Fro.

Curtis Mayfield was singing, "We're a Winner," and James Brown was shouting, "Say It Loud (I'm Black and I'm Proud)." It was the late '60s and we were a people on the move, rediscovering ourselves—long before the movement was blindsided by disco and women's lib.

We donned dashikis, wore large hooped earrings and beads, addressed each other as "brother" and "sister" (something so rare today that it almost seems foreign)—

Recognizing our commonness as an oppressed people and in relationship to our African heritage.

I grew up in the '50s and '60s, but came of age in the '70s with a sense of myself that has defined me ever since.

* * *

Been feeling quiet and melancholy lately. I think that's why I've taken to writing short vignettes about people and places from the past. It seems to be a natural inclination with the changing of the seasons, especially during the fall—something in my psyche is moved to reminisce.

I have a tendency at such times to sift through old love letters and photographs. I raise the blinds in the library so I can watch the leaves on the huge maple blush into full fall foliage...then drop like colorful parachutes jacketing the front yard. I play my favorite vinyl records that hiss and crackle and warm my spirit like a winter fire. I feel more connected to myself in the fall than in any other season.

I pull Emerson from the book shelf, along with Parks and Langston Hughes. I also have a tendency to sink into a more solitary style of expression, all of which I embrace with a familiar ease. I find that there's something about autumn that brings out the author in me on so many stereotypical levels.

I clothe myself more earnestly in the fall. Banishing the bright, colorful haberdashery of summer to an old steamer truck tucked neatly away in an upstairs' closet; I wrap my shoulders in heavy knit sweaters and light woolen overcoats and woven scarves. I slip on boots that have sat dormant throughout the summer, the musty scent of their leather a stale, familiar fragrance, and tramp through woods just beginning to change with the onset of the season. I savor autumn's cool, crisp mornings; indulge myself in her warm, languishing afternoons; and find solace in the retiring embrace of her clear, crystal, star-bright amethyst nights.

It is ritual, this changing of the seasons.

* * *

When I look at the way people talk to themselves and others, I am amazed at the negativity. We seem to have a way of diminishing people and their accomplishments with little awareness that we're even doing so. It's just the way we talk. The left-handed compliment, the snarky retort—it's like constantly playin' the dozens.

And our self-talk is even more insidious. We translate our forgetfulness into stupidity, our kindness into being weak. We downplay our looks, question our intelligence, hide our talents, and tell ourselves that we are less and can never change. We surrender our ability to believe—in ourselves and in a friendly universe.

"Our deepest fear is not that we are inadequate," writes Marianne Williamson. "Our deepest fear is that we are powerful beyond measure. It is our light, not our darkness, that which most frightens us."

"Our light not our darkness" does seem to be at the heart of the matter. I guess it's because we're told that it's not appropriate to "toot your own horn" or "pat yourself on the back." And if you do, people become offended and accuse you of being unnecessarily boastful. But "Pride" is more than just a pack of lions; its antonym an expression of satisfaction and delight in what we do and truly believe about ourselves.

These thoughts and expressions were provoked after a visit with a close friend the other night, who shared with me the unhappiness of her current life situation. Slumped uneasy in my easy-chair, she bemoaned her fate: single, college debt, a mortgage payment and job she didn't like. Overweight and unhappy, she both blamed and berated herself for her current predicament.

What I found most interesting was her confession that it mattered little that she was better off than most, or the fact that things could be worse. When juxtaposed against other folks' reality, just knowing these two things brings me immediate solace and perspective.

I don't believe in strangling hope or drowning faith. I don't believe in placing myself in a position of utter despair. Not anymore. There was a time I talked and saw things more bleakly, though not as much as many. The seed was there, planted by others and nurtured by my own faltering sense of self. But time and experience have taught me better; that my outlook about life and others plays a significant part in my ability at weathering the storm and knowing that things will be better. I just wished I could have convinced her of that.

*I wish I could show you, when you are lonely or in darkness,*
*the astonishing light of your own being.—Hafiz*

* * *

This morning, after a very arduous workout, I lay back on the weight bench as sunlight, flooding through the open porch door, bathed me in a shimmering glow of yellow light. Closing my eyes to the brightness, my lids took on a crimson blush as small blood vessels laced an intricate design across the scope of my vision. In that moment of illumination I sought revelation, and when I opened my eyes the darkness that greeted me was both clear and muted.

This morning, just after experiencing a discerning moment—I looked up into an inviting sky of faded blue, while sweat, glistening like starlight against the dark of my body, trickled down in little streams, and the cool morning air massaged my fatigued muscles like a worried lover…and a poem I had written long ago danced across the foreground of my mind:

Summer skies are turquoise
Winter skies are blue
nights we spent together
dreams we never knew
laughter in the morning
loving through the day
summer skies were in your eyes
when you went away.

Summer skies are turquoise
Winter skies are blue
sometime in the dark of night
I reach out for you
I would say I'm sorry
treat you like a friend
summer skies were in your eyes
when you left again.

Summer skies are turquoise
Winter skies are blue
all the seasons in between
come and go with you
love may not last forever
but this I know is true
summer skies are turquoise
winter skies
are blue.

I don't know what it is about poetry that sustains me. I do believe that it is confession. That within the folds of rhyme and prose I find solace, if not some form of redemption. And poems, like this one, are etched forever in memory and in the moment of the experience that created them. Back in the day when I was so much younger, writing poetry was so real and easy. It was both lonely and exciting. I don't think I'll ever be that free or innocent again.

This morning, I sought revelation, but instead was given the memory of a poem written long ago…and I wonder if they are not the same thing.

*                    *                    *

In his book *The Power of Now*, author Eckhart Tolle explains that the now moment is the only moment there is. He goes on to say (and I'm paraphrasing) that, "most of our fears and anxieties come from our projections onto the future, and most of our resentments and regrets come from our attachments to the past." We have very little control over the future and we can't do anything about the past; the only place and time we can influence is the present moment in how we think and act.

So mindfulness is all about where I place my attention; about being conscious in the present moment, and in what I think and say to myself as well as to others. Our ability to make wise choices is linked to the awareness we bring to the moment at hand. When we focus our attention on the future—on what might happen—or on the past—on what has happened—then we tend to make choices that are not always in our best interest. It is only by being rooted in the present, conscious yet oblivious, that good and right decisions are made. The more mindful I am, the more control I have over any given situation, and the more all right I'll be concerning the choices I make. Being mindful in the present makes it possible for me to have the future I desire. Full awareness means full responsibility. Learning this has literally changed my life.

*                    *                    *

As a black person, I know how important this now moment is, because we seldom have the leisure of missed opportunities. For many of us the smallest of things can be an opportunity, while for others it's simply a given. And I know in order to engage life fully, one must be unafraid of its myriad circumstances. One must be willing to encounter life on its own terms with little regard for a desired outcome—only because life is just too nuanced for any particular expectation. One must be willing, as writer Gregg Levoy so aptly put it, "*To boogie with the bogyman.*"

*                    *                    *

Living a fearless life is scary. It's scary because it demands that I put myself out there and stop playing it safe. This is true, especially at this stage of my life. Surviving the vulgarities of life is easy; it's the living afterwards that's hard. Sort of like being assaulted or robbed—one might survive the experience but, in the end, is left traumatized and fearful; afraid to step outside the door. It seems so much of our response to life these days is from a place of fear.

I want to be more than just a survivor of living. I want to be a liver of life; unafraid to hurt, or be wrong, or doubt myself. Too often we want guarantees against experiencing any of those things. We want a life devoid of doubt, heartache, and betrayal, but just to be born human is to open ourselves up to the pain and pleasure of experiencing it all.

And it turns out that there are some guarantees; they're just not the ones we want. It's guaranteed that you'll doubt yourself often and fail more times than not—that people will enter and exit your life like roommates in a college dorm. It's pretty much guaranteed that if you open your heart to love you will be hurt—but letting go and opening yourself to living improves the stakes and increases the odds that you will succeed; have friendships that last forever, and love passionately throughout the rest of your days.

*"We must be willing to get rid of the life we've planned,*
*so as to have the life that is waiting for us."*
*-Joseph Campbell*

## NOVEMBER

S M T W T F S

Early this morning a small storm-front finally arrived. I could hear the thunder booming in the distance. Then, just as faintly the rain began falling, quenching the thirst of the dry, parched land.

It's a little too late, as the leaves, deprived so long of the sweet elixir necessary for their fall changing, were knocked from the branches dry and wrinkled, their color dull and faded from dehydration.

The wind has turned from the south, as our weather has been unseasonably warm of late, and the cool, slightly chilling northern breeze is a harsh contrast to yesterday's short-sleeved, seventy-degree weather. Autumn is surrendering her last sigh of the season to winter's harsh, encroaching breath. It won't be long now.

*       *       *

Late yesterday evening, I had one of those rare moments. You know, the kind you have after sharing a deep conversation with a close friend. And after our conversation, I decided to drop the top on the car, and took a leisurely drive to a familiar lakefront.

The night air was clean and cool with just the slightest hint of humidity, and the night sky was ghostly and dark; dappled with low-hanging storm clouds and punctuated with small, bright burning stars. There was no moon.

Sitting on a bench at the edge of the lake, I thought about our conversation. I could hear the water lapping at the shallow shoreline, and in the distance, disembodied voices floated out across the dark expanse where starlight sparkled and shimmered in a gentle dance upon the waves.

I love those moments after good conversations, where ideas and intimate thoughts are shared and challenged. I love people whose passions supersede the common dogma that so often passes for enlightenment; who understand a deeper truth other than those handed down by religion and patriarchy.

I find it rare, these days, to meet people who refuse to drink the Kool-Aid; those who prefer a bolder draft, one brewed from a diversity of aspirations and imaginings. We live in a world of regurgitated thinking; crammed with worthless memes that get stamped on the envelope of our mind, then passed on from generation to generation.

Really good conversation is both challenging and comfortable, especially if it's coming from a place of communication. People who are about communicating an idea or thought are respectful of differing opinions because the goal is one of understanding, of trying to make sense of things.

It's funny, but the biggest part of communicating is listening. Listening to what is being said, and not to what we think we're hearing. This is so hard to do, because we bring so many of our insecurities to the table. It's impossible to hear another if we're defensive, angry or contemptuous. There is no conversation, only dueling perspectives, each attempting to one-up the other.

*"Good communication is as stimulating as black coffee,*
*and just as hard to sleep after."*
*-Ann Morrow Lindbergh*

* * *

It saddens me know that race plays such a prominent role in my daily life; that nearly every decision and choice is tempered by an awareness that things might in some way be affected by the color of my skin. And even more disturbing is the fact that it's so imperceptible to those who are estranged from my reality.

I say this after just having listened to an interview on NPR with the writer of the blog, Humans of New York. Out of work and wanting to do something creative that reflected his place on the planet, the author purchased a camera and began photographing and interviewing people on the streets. The results of that sudden flash of inspiration: a number one bestseller on the New York Times book list.

It had me thinking of a similar idea I had with regard to photographing the landscape of alleyways that laced my backyard neighborhood; having noticed one day while warily walking down one, all the images that lined the graveled backstreets: the texture of decaying roofs, the faded and peeling paint on aging wood sheds, the way ivy swallowed up whole fence lines, and how sunlight filtering through autumn leaves casted a lace pattern of shadows across my path—a macro world of photographs just outside my back porch door.

But the operative word in that paragraph is *warily*—because just walking down the alley, I was acutely aware of its side-yard implications. A Black man in a shadowy alleyway, peeking and prodding—even with a camera in tow, I'm suspect—and I can only imagine trying to do such a thing on the streets of New York City. Not that it's impossible, just not as easy as it would be for any white person choosing to do so.

This, I know, is the reality of my thinking, always, especially as a creative person of color. How possible is it for me to do something without being perceived that I'm up to no good?

I remember watching a popular network TV show where they create a fake but plausible situation and then see how people respond. In this particular scenario, which took place in the progressive city of Portland, Oregon, known for its bicycling populace, a situation was set up to see how people would react to a person with bolt cutters and a hacksaw attempting to free a bicycle chained to a bike rack.

In the first case a young, casually dressed white man explained to passersby that he had lost his keys and sought their assistance in cutting the lock.

Without so much as a second thought, everyone he solicited came to his aid. A young white woman placed in the same situation rendered similar results.

However, when they placed a young, casually dressed Black man in that same situation, people not only refused to assist him, but actually challenged his ownership, and took to photographing him while threatening to call the police. When confronted by the show's host, and asked if *race* had anything to do with their response, all of them insisted that it didn't. But the truth was way too obvious.

How the dominant society categorizes me will always have an impact on the things I say and do. This is at the heart of many of the police shootings of young Black men in our nation, and will continue to distort and make the country a dangerous place for me to live. Knowing this reality is beneficial in keeping me safe, but I am also saddled with the challenge to not let it hinder me in my quest for self-fulfillment.

Is it fair that I should have to approach life in this manner? No! But whoever said that life was fair?

*"Are Black men an endangered species? No. Because endangered species are protected by the law." -Chris Rock*

* * *

Identity is how people see you; it is what they place on you from the outside. Self-identity is how you see yourself; it is both what people place on you from the outside and what you make of yourself from the inside out.

Identity places me in the context of others who are like me in the most obvious ways: my ethnicity, my social economic, my political leanings, etc. My self-identity allows me to separate myself from all that stuff so as to recognize my distinctiveness from the herd of humanity—it allows me the flexibility to move in and out of my personal preferences as well as those placed on me from the outside world.

We come into this world a blank slate ready to be written on—first by our families, then by the various people who will navigate their way through our life. Like a city park outhouse or a high school locker room, not everything written on us will be of value. We live in a world full of angry pranksters, shortsighted graffiti artists and self-serving vandals—each ready to step in and teach us a wrong thing or two about what we don't know.

And then there are the things that simply happen to us...horrible things that wound our psyche and make the world unsafe. They traumatize our spirit leaving us broken and unsure about who we are or can possibly ever be. That's why having a right sense of self is so important—it protects us—swaddles us in a cloak of self-love so that we might be more self-forgiving.

Self-identity...knowing who I am...is that right sense of self.

* * *

Writer, James Baldwin once alleged, "To be Black and conscious in America, is to be constantly outraged." Believe me, there are a whole lot of unconscious Black people out there stumbling through life like the walking dead—and twice as many white folks starring in the own personal Roger Corman movie.

To be truly conscious is a cathartic yet frightening thing. In freeing myself from the lies I bought into, I bind myself to the reality of what things really are. And even more, it demands a response. It dares me to be more present in the things I do and say, and especially in the things I believe.

If I can survive living with the slightest inkling of a sense of self—wake up and be given another day at life—then I'm challenged to make things different. To use those cruel and disheartening events from the past as stepping-stones across the deep chasms constantly cleaving the earth beneath my feet; ready in an instant to dislodge my footing and send me tumbling back into the abyss.

This consciousness has made me more deft at sidestepping bad circumstances, misinformation and inflammatory rhetoric—and not to be so easily led astray of right thinking.

*"Your truth will always feel like freedom."—Martha Beck*

* * *

I am a writer and an artist. I remember learning that those were titles I needed to claim in order to make them real; that regardless of being published or purchased, those were the two things that claimed my spirit and colored how I saw and approached the larger world.

Of course, along with those things were the particulars: being Black, male and heterosexual and a whole bunch of family history…both good and bad. They give background to my claims and provide me with the experiences needed in expressing myself both creatively and individually.

I was never a follower. And I don't know how I came to simply be all right with the way I am; I only know that, somewhere, after all the angst of boyhood, and the uncertainty of early adulthood, I suddenly discovered something about myself that made it all right for me to be in the skin I'm in. This is where we all want to end up.

* * *

How strange it is (just barely weeks into November) to hear the harbinger of summer pounding at the gates of the holiday season. But there she was, insisting to be let in, brought about by a warm breeze that our local weatherman failed to predict.

* * *

With a new year loitering impatiently around the corner, I find it only fitting to begin to assess and sum up this past year of journal writing.

This was to be my year of looking back across the spectrum of my life; all the while being present in this moment that was continually unfolding before me. Few things have had the power of leading me back to myself as journaling. Especially this conscious journaling journey I had embarked upon.

I love writing. And in the past year I had come full circle in relationship to that love. When I write…when I capture my thoughts on paper…I take them from the realm of my imagination and make them more real. All the incomplete pieces of who I am or imagine myself to be come together in a more coherent shape. In writing I am made whole, and in some ways reaffirm what I know to be true about my better self. This is a very powerful thing.

* * *

There is a truth about who we are that only we will ever know. Too often, the vision we hold of ourselves is viewed through glasses stained with tears of regret. It's easy to see ourselves as flawed, damaged, lost and uncertain of our place in the general scheme of things.

Journaling realigns our sight—as writer Coleen Wainwright aptly confesses, "... even though they (journals) provided an excellent place for brain (and heart, and psyche) dump, they were mainly a map to me." And that's what this writing became: a map to me. But not me on the familiar level that I had always known; but, rather, me in the depths of the self whom I remember from my youth: all the dreams and ambitions, all the hurts and disappointments, all the secrets subconsciously linked to current behaviors and habits that haunt me to this day.

*          *          *

When I was in my early twenties I had the opportunity to purchase a car. I remember being at the dealership and sitting inside this really nice, sporty Camaro, with sleek instrumentations, plush bucket seats and stereo-quad surround sound. It had a light tan interior with a chocolate brown exterior and boasted a 350 V8 engine.

Although I could afford it, I didn't buy the car. I remember sitting there and thinking to myself: This car is too good for me. That was my first run-in with what I would later come to understand as "poverty consciousness." It is a subconscious attitude embraced by people who grow up poor or often without.

Sitting in thought this morning, I was transported back to that experience, and how it was only years later after I had tracked down the source of my thinking, that I was finally able to overcome that feeling of "undeservingness."

In his book *The Biology of Belief*, cell biologist Bruce Lipton explains how the pioneering science of Epigenetics is beginning to link our inner thoughts as well as our outer environment to our personal development as whole adults. For a long time scientists believed that our genetic makeup was fixed from birth, that basically, who we were was simply a throw of the genetic dice.

That's no longer the case. Not only is it not fixed, but this emerging science reveals that it's so fluid as to be effected by the genetics of our parents and grandparents—what they thought and felt, and even what they chose to eat.

Taking Dr. Lipton's findings to another level, author Joy DeGruy Leary, in her thought-provoking tome, *Post Traumatic Slave Syndrome*, explores the impact of slavery on the psyche of both Black and white people and, how the pathologies involved and evolved during that period of antebellum slavery, are passed down and show up in their psychological and physiological make up in disconcerting ways.

For African-Americans this pathology manifests itself in acts of intergroup aggression, and patterns of behavior based upon survival in a hostile situation. For whites it perpetuates a state of cognitive dissonance necessary in mitigating horrific acts of brutality against other human beings.

This is scary science in that it recognizes inherited behaviors passed down on a genetic level. At the same time it is incredibly liberating because such behavior is not written in stone, and is malleable by our individual stewardship.

*"What you focus on becomes your reality."-Jewel*

* * *

We take the sorrows of our youth and put them in a battered tin can that we bury in the backyard of our minds. We forget about them, lose the map as life drafts us off into the service of a much larger world. The memory gets buried deeper; covered over with the silt of life: college, our first job, getting married and having children. We move away, abandoning them to another place and time.

But this stuff of our past is never truly left behind. We excavate them in every act of uncontrollable rage, in the truths we hide concerning abuse, and in the lies we tell ourselves about the things we trusted that betrayed us in the end.

I believe Einstein was right, the universe may be "a friendly place," but our created reality is something altogether different.

* * *

What I have come to realize is that one needs to develop a personal philosophy about living; a way of understanding and engaging the world that edifies and is uniquely your own.

For me, as a Black writer and artist, this is so important. Without a proper philosophy, I fool myself into believing that things are no different for me than they are for others, which is both true and not. This is the paradox of being Black in America and, to some extent, of being human.

*                    *                    *

There are some truths that have stayed the same, and there are some truths that I once thought I knew that are no longer so. Depending on what I discern in this moment, most truths are subjective, and what yesterday was an absolute; is made questionable by the input of additional experiences and events. Understanding this has made a huge impact on what I believe.

*                    *                    *

The sad truth is that racism complicates the world—not just for some, but for all of us. And I place the blame squarely on the shoulders of the Western world, and white America in particular, for its dogged effort at supporting a system of White Supremacy based upon colonialism and slavery.

The belief in Manifest Destiny that supported European expansion into "undeveloped" territories was a virus of unequalled arrogance. But the racism created here in our country was a unique cancer that the white majority purposely took to spreading throughout the rest of the world.

It's well-documented that slavery, as a means of supplying free labor for nation building, was a well-established occurrence throughout most of early civilization. However, it took America, in its warped genius, to take it one step further by imposing a new model that denied the humanity of other human beings. This was a true game-changer, and it has affected the lives of Black people all over the planet.

My challenge today is not to be lead astray by this peculiar design. To recognize and understand that I am both slave and free man to these notions of the past.

*"People are trapped by history, and history is trapped in them."*
*-James Baldwin*

# DECEMBER

S M T W T F S

Coming full circle.

*　　　　*　　　　*

Regardless of all the unfairness in the world concerning the color of my skin and the history attached to it, it is my prerogative—no, scratch that—my responsibility to not let it hamper me in my efforts to be an autonomous and fully authentic human being. A human being who embraces the reality of who he is in all its complexity.

*　　　　*　　　　*

In Costa Rica they have a saying, "Pura vida!" which means "Pure life!" I like that. And that's how I intend to address my life this approaching year, and for all the years to come: purely…simply…with an acute awareness of both the past and future. But always to be present in this now moment.

*"In the end, it's what you learn after you think you know it all that counts."-Me*

# EPILOGUE:
## After Words

*"So here I am, blacker than I've ever been. But above all, Human — a condition I share with everyone of every hue.*
*I feel. I trust. I cry."*
*—Leanita McClain*

never realized how much of me would be revealed in compiling this journal. I never realized how much I resented having to view the world through the prism of my skin color, and yet, what a defining and saving grace it is to do so. Even though I started out wanting to construct a simple narrative about my love of writing, and the impact that it's had on my development (I think I achieved that somewhat throughout the first part of the manuscript), I soon realized that in journaling there was simply no way to escape viewing the world through the dark lens of my Blackness.

It was there at nearly every turn—a part of each and every encounter no matter how innocent or benign. And it was such a subtle thing; a habit and way of being in the world that I had become so accustomed to—a slight here, an impertinence there, a left-handed comment wrapped in the veneer of something far more telling and sinister. It was about more than my place in the world; it was about my place in a world that was often uncomfortable with me.

It surprised me how even the most mundane circumstances were back-storied by events and memories that complicated their unfolding. It was tiring to say the least, and that was the most telling thing of all: the fatigue that came with always being on guard, the constant questioning of one's self and others made it hard to write about life in its most mundane manner, in simply enjoying the everyday virtues of being alive.

There were times when I was able to capture small moments of intimate grandeur, in the way sunlight entered a room, or how a thin swirl of clouds framed the sky on a purple starry night; or simply sharing the insights and trappings of being unbearably human. And I found that I lived for those moments when race and ethnicity didn't matter...those moments we all know and experience that reinforce the understanding that we are more alike than not—but all too often the dark specter of our nation's history would creep into the room, casting a hard edge shadow across my consciousness.

I discovered that it was impossible for me to not see the world through an Afrocentric perspective. Not only was it impossible, but it was neither honest nor healthful.

There is an "otherness" to being Black that cannot be denied—as a person of color you know this. There is the awareness that no matter how much better things are in comparison to the past, something is still amiss; that despite the progress, there are things on a very human level that have never really changed.

*"Just because everything is different, doesn't mean that anything has changed."-Irene Peter*

In an interview broadcasted by Kansas City University Radio, Christian Rudder, co-founder of *Ok Cupid*, a popular online dating site and author of the book, *Dataclysm: Who We Are When We Think No One's Looking*, talked openly about what some of the statistics he collected revealed about the American public. Despite the favorable responses people gave when polled about interracial relationships, their online dating antics show a completely different pattern—underscoring our ambivalence concerning race, and indicative of the old joke: "I don't have a problem with mixed relationships, as long as it's not in my family."

Human beings, regardless of their ethnicity, are still the same genus. Unlike cats and dogs, which are totally different species—we are a mixture of colors and appearances based upon geography, culture and myriad things that make us both common and distinct. We breed among our differences with relative ease, and with little fear that the union (if not closely blood-related) will produce a two-headed offspring with a third eye that favors its father. Yet, despite this understanding, we have an extremely difficult time accepting it.

Life is dichotomous; there's no getting around it. Night/day, black/white, good/evil, male/female; one can go on and on—opposites but not always opposing, at least not within the context of enlightenment. There are no contradictions in the dichotomy of this way of thinking. It's possible for us to be both satisfied and discontent, and for other things to be both literal and mystical, secular and spiritual; known and yet filled with the unraveling of mystery. However, enlightenment doesn't stem from the denial of reality. Enlightenment comes from confronting reality no matter how painful and unforgiving the consequences. For Black folks this has always been difficult because assimilation (our prerequisite to the American Dream) robs us of our right mind.

Assimilation has you looking at the world through eyes that aren't your own; through circumstance and habits that do not reflect or define you properly. It is the wholesaling of your cultural consciousness…your very essence…in an effort to satisfy a "different other."

But the real sin in the story is our inability to look beyond the lie in its telling; to accept and believe wholeheartedly in the myths we create about each other, all the while disregarding the nuances involved, that our realities are similar but not the same, which is okay, but only if we're willing to acknowledge it.

In January of 2015, President Barack Obama came under criticism for comments made at an annual prayer breakfast where he chided Christians not to be so smug in their condemnation of Islamic extremists, noting that Christianity had its own historical extremes when it came to race and ethnicity. The outcry from Obama's remarks came from a place of indignation that he would make such a comparison—never mind the fact that what he voiced was historically accurate and true.

The denial of a historical context is a reoccurring theme in the reality of most Black people's lives; laying groundwork in the political constructs for claims of reverse discrimination, and the off-handed dismissal of white privilege so prominent in today's discourse.

Race is a Eurocentric concept—I had to get real about that, because in many indigenous languages there was no word for race. The Lakota people of the upper northern plains, after encountering the European French, referred to them as the "Wasicheu," which literally translated into: "the greedy one who takes the fat." They viewed the European French as a people who took not only what was valuable, but also that which was of no value—leaving very little, if nothing, for others.

The same can be said of indigenous African people, who, in encountering the European, welcomed him openly onto their continent, only to suffer dire consequences. The truth in these matters is evident: When a people who have no word for race (a designation of one's humanity based upon skin pigmentation), encounters a people who do, they are instantly disadvantaged, and all that they are is held to a different standard.

American racism is unique in its reference to people of color, and in particular to people of African descent, because few other relationships between human beings have been as contentious as that which exists between Black and white people here in these United States.

*"The trouble with the world is not that people know too little,*
*but that they know so many things that ain't so."*
*—Mark Twain*

This isn't simply about slavery. Throughout history, and on nearly every continent on the planet, people have enslaved others, but what made slavery in America different was the creation of a category that took away the very humanity of another, reducing them to nothing more than chattel property—something to be owned, not known. It was a way of justifying the treatment of others in order to support a republic based on the profit from their labor.

To deny another's humanity for such a reason, is a denial of reality. And it's the denial of our reality (as an enslaved people and its inherent legacy) that is a continuous problem for a "different other." If memory is fiction, then the history of our country is a vain attempt at writing the "great American novel"; one consisting of grand discoveries and epic battles against uncivilized hordes of red and brown indigenous people—built upon the broken backs and stolen legacy of enslaved black African people—and finally sold and swallowed, hook, line and sinker by the dominant white society as a manifested fact.

"*We hold these truths, to be self-evident, that all men are created equal.*" So began the first great lie in the scripting of America's constitution. And indeed it was a scripting, as in a play, and acted out on the grand stage of nation building. From that very moment everything became suspect, as history is told from the conqueror perspective, and always at the expense of the conquered.

This is not an indictment of a select group of people; this is an indictment of an attitude, at its best, inherited by default, and at its worst, a conscious perspective erected upon the false principles of racial superiority.

Like President Obama, the words I write here may be reviled and misconstrued as lacking love of country, but in all sincerity it's nothing if not the opposite. Black History is American History—but it hasn't always been rendered so. It is a history intricately woven into the very fabric of our country and is as American as sweet potato pie—from the moment Christopher Columbus set sail with a navigator of African heritage, to the first life given in an act of Revolution *(Crispus Attucks)* — yet still, Black folks have always had a difficult time reconciling their patriotism with the country's history.

I know for a long time I felt no claim to American citizenship. Like Malcolm X and Muhammad Ali, who before me questioned the validity of our country's founding principles, I too felt little allegiance. It's hard to claim such a thing when all around you the larger society is treating you otherwise.

But America is my country! It is the country that my slave ancestors built, and my father and others of color fought for on battlefields both here and abroad, and not to claim it for their ounce of flesh is to do them a great disservice.

So, with all this coming to light in my daily expositions, I found it necessary to include an epilogue, knowing that my prologue was incomplete and devoid of certain considerations.

Writing is language in its most tangible form. And who defines me, and how they define me in a language that, intrinsically, is not my own, was an emerging caveat. But how I defined myself in that same inherited tongue was even more crucial.

Words matter. White teenagers hanging out on corners late at night "loiter"; Black teenagers "lurk." In confrontations with the police: white people get "shot"; Black people get "shot up"— nearly the same words, but with two different meanings and outcomes.

These subtle differences in verbiage matter, because they ascribe a subtle shift in individual perspective and perception. Like any writer who has ever lifted a pen in an attempt to communicate or entertain, who I am was all I had to offer in serving up something real, true, and, lastly, universal.

In his seminal writing, *The Souls of Black Folk*, Civil Rights activist W.E.B. Du Bois wrote extensively about this thing--this *"double consciousness"* that plagues the thinking of most African-Americans. It's a way of viewing the world through two sets of eyes: one, from the perspective of the dominant society's; the other from the standpoint of one's own reality. It's a schizophrenic way of looking at the world, to be sure, cloaked in the lies we tell ourselves about how race and ethnicity don't matter in the normal scheme of things. But in all reality we know it does. For black folks to ignore this double perspective is to set ourselves up for a lifetime of disappointment and

Misunderstanding—not only of ourselves, but of others, especially those who differ from us in both ethnicity and history.

A lot of people like to think it very PC to say they don't see color; they're quick to declare that it doesn't matter whether you're blue, green or purple. And they're right; it doesn't, because there are no blue, green or purple people. But there are black and white, red, yellow and brown people with a whole bunch of history attached to those color designations.

I've often wondered why some find it necessary to not acknowledge the color of my skin in order to see me as a human being? Just to believe so is to perpetuate the idea that there is still something inherently wrong with me. If anything, since White is the absence of color, it should be the other way around; that when I look at *them* I don't see color. But that would be just as erroneous. We should be able to see each other in our totality and come to know that we are all undeniably human.

To ignore that very real part of me is to expunge the history intimately tied to it, which, once again, easily supports the rejection of affirmative reparations, and the frequently challenged assertions of white privilege.

I love being Black. In a perfect world I should never have to say this because I believe that each of us, if we are somewhat healthy and secure, would readily claim the truth of who we are—with little need for public disclosure—but that's not the world we live. In America it will always be about race as long racism is used to define the pecking order in people's lives. And until we actually can come to terms with this, it will continue to impact our lives and how we understand ourselves as a diverse nation.

In journaling, I discovered two very important things. The first was that, there was a hierarchy in how I perceived myself, and the order of that hierarchy surprised me. That I was Black, or a person of African descent was my first reality, and for me to ignore that reality was, once again, to set myself up for a whole bunch of disappointment and misunderstanding.

This was a forced reality, and not the one of my choice, because I would much rather simply see myself as just another human being (the second tier in that hierarchy), but racism doesn't allow me that freedom. Though explicitly tied together, racism never allows me to step outside the territory of my skin and into the landscape of my humanness, because it denies that part even exists.

*"I realize that I'm Black, but I like to be viewed as a person, and this is everybody's wish."*
*-Michael Jordan*

I am a Black man. Not enough in our society has changed for me yet to live outside that context. However, the trick, I realized, was to be both Black and human—to respect the dictates of reality—that the color of my skin does matter in a hundred thousand ways, both outside and within the context of my character. This makes it possible for me to deal with that "double consciousness" of being Black in a white world that all too often wants to deny me that reality.

That your reality may not be my truth is something that every Black person comes to understand at a very young age. To be sure, there comes a point when one discovers that there are actually three truths regarding his/her place on the planet, and that this too has a hierarchy.

First off, there is the World's truth. This is the reality of your place in humanity's peeking order, made up from the small deaths and prejudices of our world histories. It is a biased truth, no doubt, but no less real in its influence on our lives.

Then there's Your truth. This is the truth of who you are...physically, individually. All the stuff of your life experiences that culminates in making you...you. This too is a biased truth, but only in the sense that it's not fixed.

And finally there is a Universal truth. This is the truth of physics...that the sun rises in the east and sets in the west, that what goes up must come down, that regardless of gender, ethnicity or orientation, we are still the same species on this planet circling the sun.

It's necessary for Black folks to recognize the hierarchy of these truths in order to deal effectively with the circumstances of their daily lives. You can get really thrown off balance if you get this wrong, and go off into the world thinking you are something other than what reality dictates. This happens all the time with biracial children who believe they are someone other than how they are perceived by a biased world. Or affluent Black kids raised in all white neighborhoods and attending overpriced private schools in exclusive communities. You might think yourself unique and equal up until the point that someone, in referencing you, uses the N-word.

Even more, there is a absurdity that lies at the heart of understanding these truths, and that is, in order to deal with them successfully, one must see them

In their particular order, but brave them in reverse.

They must be engaged from the basis of our universal truth that we are all human beings, that our shared humanity is the stuff of our individual character, and gives credence to our uniqueness as persons of a particular genus. And from our diverse perspective we are called to challenge the status quo; in the way the larger world has been made to work against us.

*"All people know the same truth. Our lives consist of how we choose to distort it."-Robin Williams (Deconstructing Harry)*

Why is this important?

Because I am writing this at a time when young Black men and women are dying at an unprecedented rate, in situations both extraneous and mundane: for panhandling cigarettes and CDs, for broken tail lights and jaywalking; for failure to answer commands given without full disclosure, or reaching to comply with instructions yelled out from accosting law enforcers; for failing to understand that the reality of the world's truth, trumps their individual truth…when "living while Black."

We all, not just Black folks, live within the context of these truths. And we are all subjugated to their hierarchy whether we acknowledge it or not.

That everything has a context is the greatest understanding we can give ourselves in coming to grips with the behavior of a biased society. We readily forget that we are a species who only recently have emerged from the shadows of the cave; that we are mere novices to the precepts of civilization; and that our technology has outstripped and outsourced our human development.

There was a time when we lived in what was once referred to as an "agricultural society," which later became an "industrial society," each honoring the fact that the human element was paramount.

Moving into a "technological age" redefined that. It shifted the focus from a "society" that had been defined by its institutions and culture, into a more gilded and sterile "age" which came to be defined mainly by its achievements.

Those achievements happened to be in the realm of the material; so, it comes as no surprise that our families would move from "extended," which embraced our humanity to the inclusion of others, to "nuclear," which seems to embrace our technology to the exclusion of everyone else.

This move from a "society" to an "age" was actually more of a quantum leap with several far-reaching implications we've yet to take notice of. The mere use of the term "quantum" is to denote an abrupt change, a complete break from an ideal or thought previously known or considered.

The societal elements of who we were will never be again, as the "age" into which we have progress has fully established itself.

Today we wallow in the throes of an "Information age"—which is truly misleading—information is not knowledge. It's been said that we are a culture "drowning in information and starving for knowledge." Indeed. In these times, where technology has outstripped human development, we find ourselves once more at odds with each other; lacking in our capacity to care.

It's a historical default that we, as a nation, fall into with very little realization that it could be any other way. That the notion of white superiority, coupled with a sense of entitlement is real, and very much ingrained; a well-worn habit...a casual adherence to a flawed point of view, and as virulent as any untreated disease.

It is a sense of privilege edified by a worldview that is historic in its magnitude and, like drug addiction, one not easily overcome by just saying "No."

There is a riot going on in the hearts of white Americans today. Although many of us might choose to disbelieve it, most white people really do care, but are in constant conflict with the way things are and the way things used to be. Caught up in the changing politics and the confusing protocol of the last fifty years, they find themselves severely at odds with the changes taking place.

Privilege has its own curse. And for most, the blight of racial bias is like the mark of Cain firmly stamped upon the forehead of their psyche. Cursed to wander the landscape of social affairs, they find themselves driven from confrontation to confrontation, conflicted with the knowledge that they're supposed to be their brothers' keepers.

*"Be nice to whites, they need you to rediscover their humanity."*
*-Bishop Desmond Tutu*

There's a revolution going on, and this time it can't help but be televised, downloaded and flashed across the internet for all to see. It will not be qualified by any act of Congress, nor legislated into compliance. It has to take place in the heart, its onus the responsibility of every woman and man.

What I am talking about is a revolution in both mind and spirit; a wholehearted acknowledgment of our entrenched misperceptions of the past, and a sincere effort at reconstituting the future.

This is not revisionist rhetoric. Nor an apologetic appeal for the crimes of our forefathers. As the late author and poet Maya Angelou was fond of saying, "When you know better...you do better." History and its circumstances will always be an undeniable part of our present-day reality.

Still, if we fail (through hard-headedness and vain attempts at saving face) to honestly redress the mistaken concepts of the past as it pertains to Black people and others of color, then we will never have the peace we seek. Though we may give the appearance of having moved beyond the rhetoric, we will remain forever hostage to negotiations of the heart; our children heirs to a kingdom barred from kindred kindness, and our society imprisoned behind barbed words of disrespect and stonewalled misunderstandings.

Within the body of creation beats a heart of enormous compassion...capable of rendering great art in canvas and stone, and inspiring movements in dance and music.

It is the pulsing of this heart that has pushed men/women to scale mountains; to lay track across the surface of an entire continent, and erect huge edifices of concrete and steel that give witness to their genius.

Within that same body, however, beats a heart of unimaginable cruelty; capable of lying waste to both man and beast and indifferent to the suffering of others.

It is the pounding of this heart that has pierced the soul of heaven with its heinous acts of wars, with its lust for wealth and power that has devastated whole cultures and landscapes, and made impossible the peace of the world.

We must remind ourselves of the need to reach back across the historical divide and reconnect with one another. "What is required of us," writes the poet Raymond Broughan, "is that we break open our blocked caves and find each other...nothing less will heal the anguished spirit...nor release the heart to act in love."

*"The moment we cease to hold each other, the moment we break faith with one another, the sea engulfs us and the light goes out."*
*—James Baldwin*

Printed in the United States
By Bookmasters